For people in projects

Invented and edited, with love and passion, in Berlin / Germany.

Copyright © 2017 by Frank Habermann & Karen Schmidt. All rights reserved.

No part of this publication may be reproduced, stored in a retrieval system, or transmitted in any form or by any means, electronic, mechanical, photocopying, recording or otherwise, without the prior written permission of the authors.

Limit of Liability/Disclaimer of Warranty: While the authors have used their best efforts in preparing this book, they make no representations or warranties with respect to the accuracy or completeness of the contents of this book and specifically disclaim any implied warranties of merchantability or fitness for a particular purpose. No warranty may be created or extended by sales representatives or written sales materials. The advice and strategies contained herein may not be suitable for your situation. You should consult with a professional where appropriate. The authors shall not be liable for any loss of profit or any other commercial damages, including but not limited to special, incidental, consequential, or other damages.

This publication is part of the "Over the Fence" book project.
For more information visit overthefence.com.de

ISBN 978-3-00-055576-3

Version 1.1.
Printed in Berlin.
Layout, typesetting and final artwork by Ann-Kathrin Gallheber
Produced and distributed by Stattys.com

Project
DESIGN
**THINKING TOOLS
FOR VISUALLY SHAPING NEW VENTURES**

overthefence.com.de/the-book

A simple path to benefit from x-disciplinary knowledge,
design, manage, and lead projects, and have more fun at work.

released
2014

released
2016

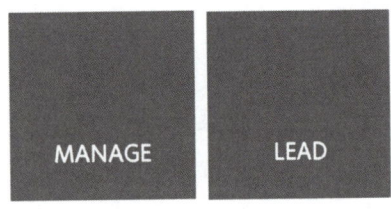

planned   planned

DESIGN is the 2nd part of the "Over the Fence"
BOOK PROJECT

What's "Over the Fence"?
Founded in 2013, "Over the Fence" is an open-source initiative for people in projects. We aim to provide the most valuable knowledge for anyone, who faces projects and is looking for hands-on tools. We are inspired by cross-disciplinary knowledge and a whole lot of common sense. Our motto is "simple but powerful – demystified and buzzword-free"!

Why are you publishing step by step?
Nobody knows everything. This is particularly true for the authors of this book. Going step by step allows us to learn and adapt to your needs. For each stage of publication, you are invited to share your thoughts, practices, and stories. Tell us, whether the content was helpful, how we could become better, and what you would like to see in the upcoming releases.

5 reasons to read this book
even if you are an experienced project manager or an absolute beginner

Project design is more than a tool book. It's a book about people in projects – how we effectively collaborate and have more fun at work.

#1
it's a simple path
It's easy to adopt some (more) effective tricks that enrich your magic kit.

#2
it helps to jump over the fence
You will acquire wisdom and powerful practices across disciplines and you will be able to blend them skillfully.

#3
it saves time
You will learn to overcome business buzzwords, understand the untold management secrets and focus on the things that really count.

#4
it's universal
Most of the presented concepts in this book are useful not only in project management, but also in general management and outside of business.

#5
it can boost your career
The presented concepts help you to better understand the diverse "people in projects" (from the bosses to "alien" experts). Bonding with people from different (working) cultures makes you a highly regarded person.

Acknowledgements

We are not claiming to be "tool gurus", neither are we the most experienced project managers. More than anything, we are listeners, observers and explorers. If you like anything in this book, it's due to the brilliant people we had the pleasure to meet. These people come from very different fields – sports, arts, crafts, engineering, education, sciences, civial society and business – and they all share a great passion for what they are doing. Before we start, we wish to thank the following persons who – consciously or unconsciously – acted as role models, sources of inspirations, and mental sparring partners for this book.

Friederike Lilien Abitz
Paulina Patricia Acuña Fernández
Dietmar Albrecht
Frédéric André
Pascale Arndtz
Mary Alice Arthur
Ria Baeck
Heiko Bartlog
Malte Beinhauer
Yan Bello
Sabine Bernhard
Birgit Bernt
Marcus Birkenkrahe
Sean Blair
Jean-Christophe Blondiau
Justus Boeckheler
Ulf Brandes
Eike Brechlin
Valentina Catena
Claudio Chesi
Eric Cornuel
Jane Cowan

Patrick D. Cowden
Alexandra Dauch
Christian De Neef
Jonathan Dubuque
Katrin Elster
Katrin Faensen
Jörg Fehlinger
Benno Fürmann
Jürgen Galler
Christoph Gast
Julian Geuder
Frauke Godat
Carolina Gorosito
Johannes Götzinger
Julia Gunnoltz
David Gurteen
Jens Hagemeyer-Lee
Deborah Hartmann Preuss
Wiebke Herding
Dirk Heuschen
Christoph Hinske
Andreea Hirica
Jens Hoffmann

Michelle Holliday
David Hudnut
Annett Irmer
Karolina Iwa
Inge Jansen
Johanna Jester
Oana Juncu
Sven Kayser
Eugene Kelly
Michael Kempf
Claudia Klar-Lustermann
Stefanie Klein
Sue Knight
Yorgos Konstantinou
Mario Konzag
Wolfgang Kraemer
Michael Kraus
Janina Kugel
Jan Langebartels
Diana Larsen
Jens Lillebæk
Dominik Ludwig
Eric Lynn

Anne Madsen
Elizabeth Maloba
Mikko Mannila
Oliver Masucci
Frank Milius
Giulia Molinengo
Eugenio Molini
Roland Müller
Rainer Müller
Roman Muth
Holger Nauheimer
Pierre Neis
Sabine Norek
Sebastien Paquet
Niels Pfläging
Vittoria Piattelli
Sven Pohland
Soledad Pons Caruso
Garry Pugliese
Stefanie Quade
Belina Raffy
Marianna Recchia
Roland Rolles

Patrick Roth
Hansjörg Sand
Andreea Sava
Otto Scharmer
Joschi Scharmer-Yu
Vera Scharmer-Yu
August-Wilhelm Scheer
Peter A. Schmidt
Madlen Serban
Sabine Soeder
Egon Steinkasserer
Adam StJohn Lawrence
Antje Traue
Arne van Oosterom
Brigitta Villaronga
Sébastién Visentin
Sebastian Völz
Christoph Wargitsch
Volker Wiegmann
Martin Wilhelm
Lynne Ann Williams
Nancy Wright White

- Developing a new leadership model
- Re-allocating the sales force
- Re-building the city
- Creating a research study
- Outsourcing
- Aiming for ISO certification
- Opening a subsidiary in a new market
- Introducing the new controlling management
- Inventing a service
- Setting-up a data warehouse
- Jointly writing a fantastic book
- Merging companies
- Providing development aid
- Recreating employer brand
- Developing a strategy for corporate social responsibility
- Implementing business software
- Finding an agency for the marketing campaign
- Moving to another office building
- Improving the material management system

DESIGN

"DESIGN" is where you learn to form and shape your project. Designing a project is a process of careful consideration and iterative reflection. It gives you insights to what your project means and what your project needs.

The Project Canvas is a foundational instrument for designing a project. "DESIGN" provides you with a variety of additional thinking tools, which complement your project design kit.

Benefit from surprisingly simple techniques and visual templates, which have proven to be helpful for many people. With these few instruments you are able to tailor a powerful design for your project – a design that helps you to master your challenge!

TABLE OF CONTENTS

FOUNDATIONS — 13

A project is... — 16
This is project design — 18
Ten principles of good project design — 22

PROCEDURE — 24

Occasions for project design — 26
Essential project design — 30
In-depth project design — 50

LESSONS FOR A GOOD PROJECT DESIGN — 56

Project purpose and output (lessons 1 to 6) — 58
The 3 schools of project thinking (mental side trip) — 86
Project procedure and input (lessons 7 to 12) — 92
The art of scoping (mental side trip) — 126
Project goals and environment (lessons 13 to 18) — 130
Closing time (lessons 19 to 23) — 150

LASTLY — 176

References — 177
Solutions to the riddles — 180
More resources from "Over the Fence" for your great projects — 184

**EVERY GREAT PROJECT
BEGINS WITH
A REALLY GOOD
DESIGN**

A GAME IS...

... a space where the rules of ordinary life are temporarily suspended and replaced with the rules of the game. In fact, a game creates an alternative world, a model world."
[Gray et al., Gamstorming 2010, p.1]

A PROJECT IS...

... a space where the rules of everyday working life are temporarily suspended and replaced with the rules of the project. In fact, a project creates an alternative world, a project world.

This is Project Design

Projects, just as games, are out of the ordinary. They are temporary sidesteps from daily obligations, routines, and structures. Projects as well as games ask for a special arrangement of time, space, participants, and rules. This special arrangement is what we call "the design"!

The design of a project can be fairly basic or very sophisticated; it can be informally arranged or formally set out in writing. However the case, an effective design always needs the commitment of all "players". If people don't like their playground, if they don't accept or understand the rules of play, the desired action cannot take place (or it won't be fun at all).

The project canvas is your tool to systematically design a new project. When a project is to be started, people typically have a different understanding about the project. This is due to professional views, personal interests, cultural backgrounds and many reasons more. The canvas helps you to deal with these diverse starting points, facilitate communication and develop a common ground. In this book, you receive a number of "thinking tools", which support and leverage your work with the project canvas.

While in general, design is the conscious effort to create a meaningful order, project design is the collaborative effort to create a meaningful order that makes sense for each person involved.

"Design is the conscious effort
to impose a meaningful order."

— Victor Papanek, advocate of responsible design

1. Any project design is better than no project design.
2. A good project design is better than a bad project design.
3. The best project design is a commonly agreed project design.

1. Each project has some sort of a design. If you deny its existence or if you are not aware of it, you may face serious problems. Therefore, know the design criteria of your project and actively work on it.

2. A tailored project design obviously is better than a standard design which does not entirely meet the specifics of your project. Learn the lessons of a good project design and set up a high-quality project.

3. The impact and resilience of your project design is the greatest, if it is agreed among all project members. Within the design process, engage the knowledge of everybody and aim for genuine participation.

10 PRINCIPLES

OF GOOD PROJECT DESIGN

Good project design is ...

eye-opening
Designing your project is a process of exploration and consideration. It inevitably gives insights into what your project means and what your project needs.

lean
Good project design makes few and very clear statements. It neither needs many words nor further explanations.

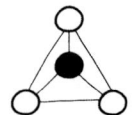
holistic
Though lean, good project design covers every crucial aspect of your project; it comprises all project building blocks as well as their relationships.

purposeful
Good project design never is an end in itself; it is set up to reach the purpose of your project and deliver value to the customer.

efficient
Good project design requires an economically reasonable effort. The bigger your project, the more you can invest in its design.

individual
Good project design is as individual as your project – it is tailored to your challenge and your situation.

understandable
Good project design is guided by a unifying scheme of language, symbols, and patterns, which are understood by all project participants.

agreed
Good project design provides a single point of view, which is accepted by project participants from diverse professions and cultures.

resilient
Good project design provides a robust yet flexible setting that can cope with future changes.

good-enough-for-now
Good project design is temporary and pragmatic. It is tied to its moment of use and helps the project to enter the next level.

OCCASIONS FOR

PROJECT DESIGN

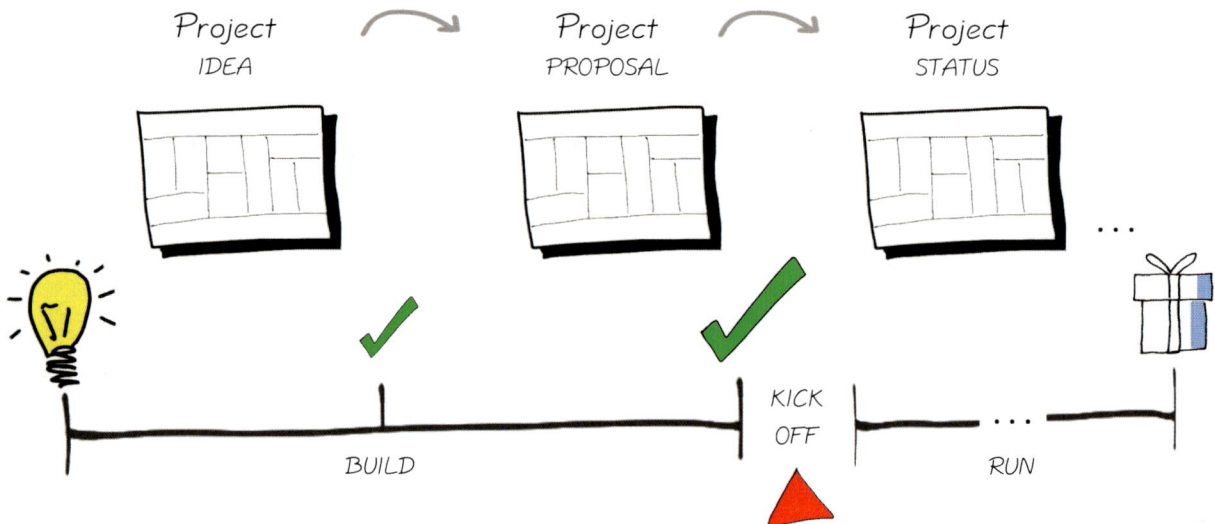

Occasions for Project Design

Project design happens due to various reasons and during various project stages. This is particularly true for complex projects, which are designed and re-designed multiple times. The picture on the left illustrates design events, which are typical for the life cycle of any bigger project. Since the re-design of an already running project applies the same techniques as project design during build time, we focus on these two events:
– design of the project IDEA
– design of the project PROPOSAL

Project IDEA Design:
Many people have great ideas. But often, an idea is not enough to start an ambitious project. Usually, you want to think through your idea and map out related constraints and impacts, before you kick-off your venture. This is the first stage of project design. By means of the project canvas and a set of powerful thinking tools, you can gain and visualize your first holistic picture of the project. This result is helpful to gain confidence, supporters and sponsors, and enter the next stage.

Project PROPOSAL Design:
Bigger projects need a sound preparation. The stage between the idea sketch and the actual start of the project is called "project description", "feasibility study", or "business case analysis". Not rarely, this stage is so comprehensive that it becomes an own project, a so-called "pre-project". The main result of such a pre-project is the "Project Design". Based on your visual project design, further project documents can be issued (if needed), and the project can start.

ESSENTIAL

PROJECT DESIGN

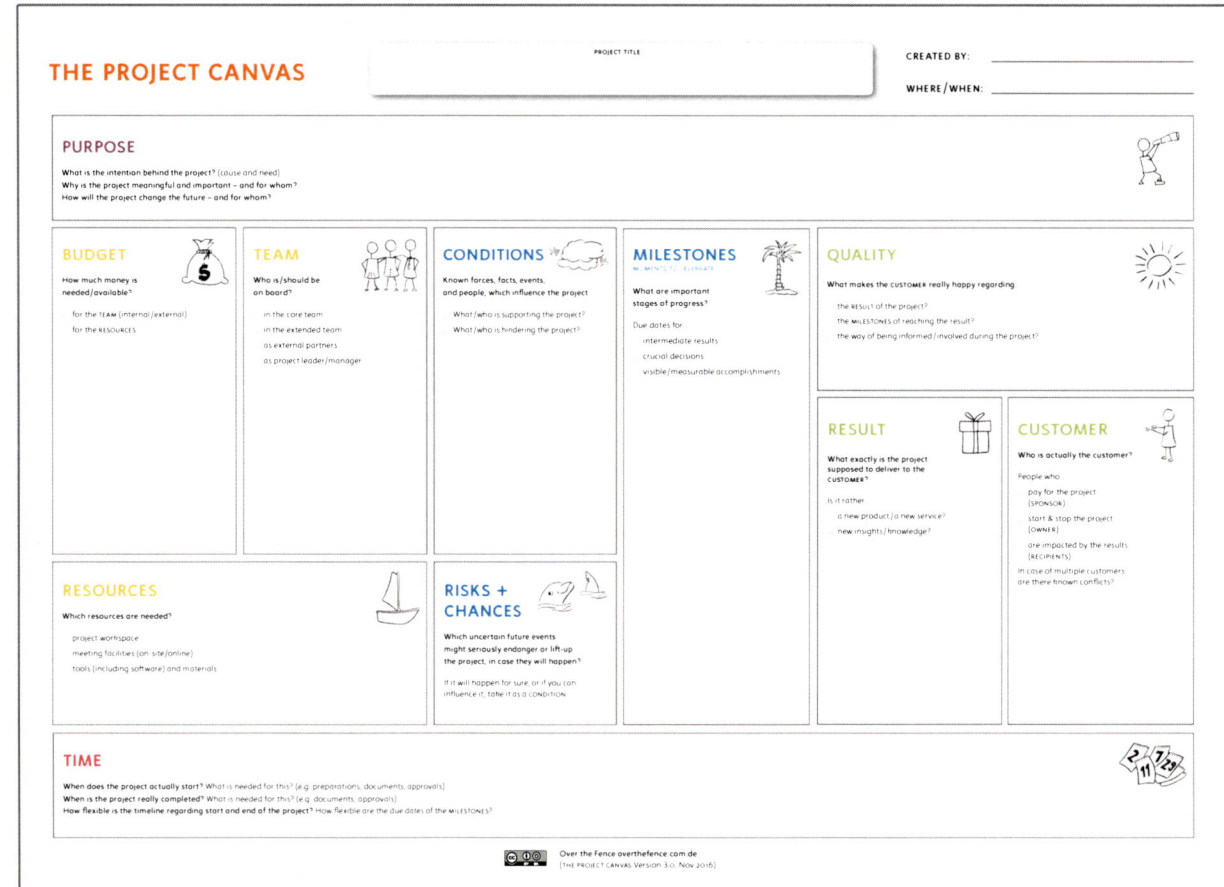

Download for free at overthefence.com.de/project-canvas

Apply the Project Canvas

The Project Canvas allows you to design your project on one page!

For your essential project design, you can simply download the Project Canvas from the "Over the Fence" website, follow the handy tips given there, and utilize the tool for your purposes.

For more information, explore the CANVAS book.

next pages →
people applying the Project Canvas

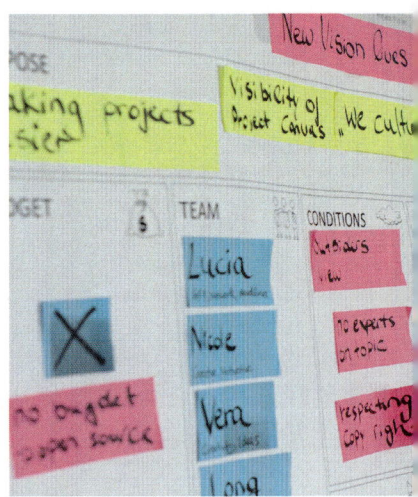

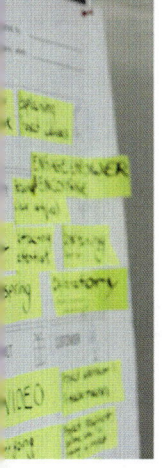

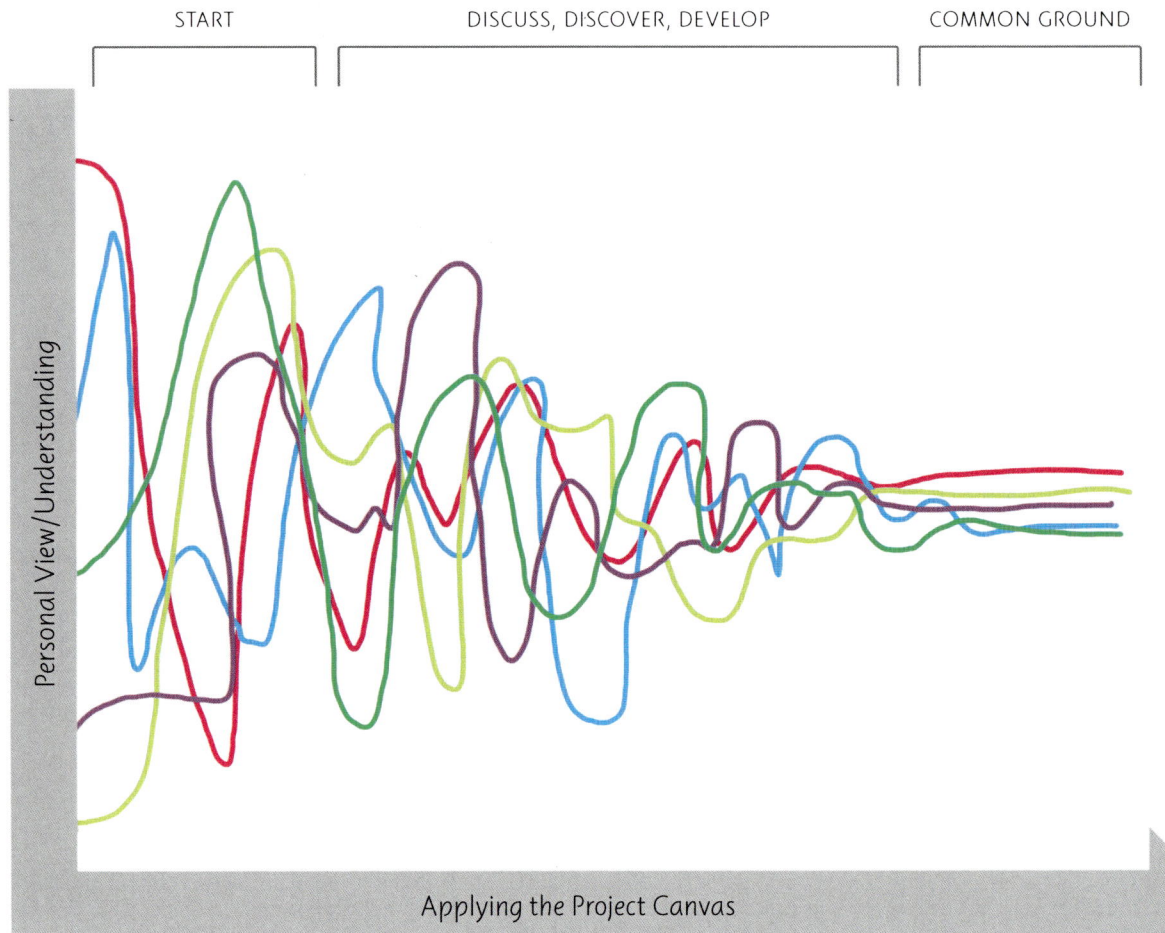

Magic Conversations (Part I)

When people ask us, "what's actually the Project Canvas?", our answer is, **"it's a sheet of paper, that serves as an invitation to talk"**. And that's true. More than anything, the project canvas is an excuse to break away from daily routines and take the time to discuss a project.

Everybody can observe the magic that happens, when people gather around their canvas. This magic is created by what Yves Pigneur and Alexander Osterwalder call the "design attitude". For some people, particularly in big organizations, the design attitude is the exact opposite of the linear decision-oriented approach they are used to. Having a design attitude means taking time for open-minded and non-linear analysis and exploration.

Since the project canvas provides guidance too, this exploration is neither chaotic nor undirected. Quite the contrary, it's clear and systematic.

But the project canvas is not a cook book; it does not provide a strict instruction. It is weakly structured and therefore leaves room for each team to find their own way. This is another ingredient of the magic: when applying the project canvas people discuss, discover, develop and through this find a common ground.

The picture on the left illustrates this. At the beginning of the design process, the individual views concerning the project are very different. This is normal at the beginning of every complex project. It's not because some people are "wrong or right", it's just because of diverse professional and cultural perspectives and divergent states of information. It's because, we all live "in different worlds". But then, when applying the canvas, magic happens and **people create a shared picture of their project, a common project world**.

"In the same environment, everyone lives in a different world."
__ Arthur Schopenhauer, The Wisdom of Life

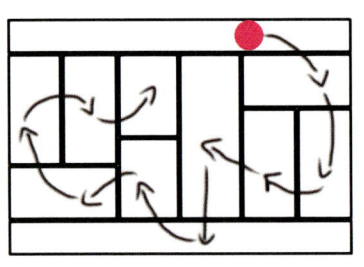
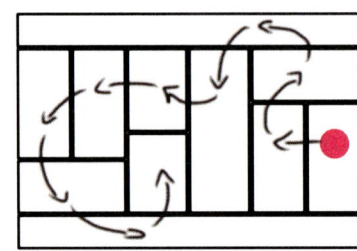
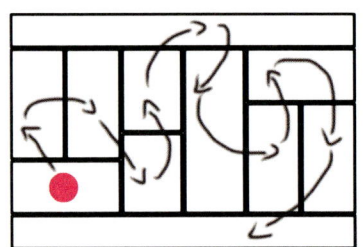

Just a few of
39.916.800
ways to design a project

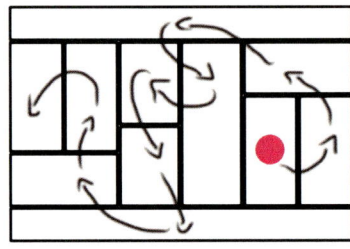
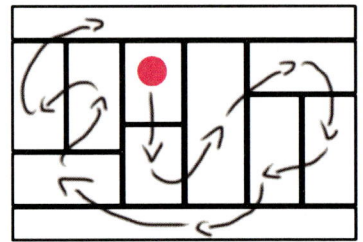
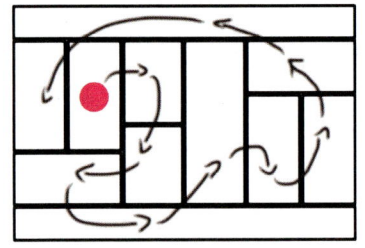

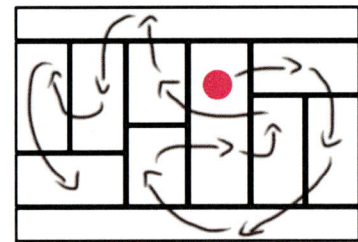
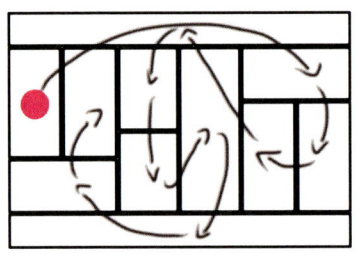
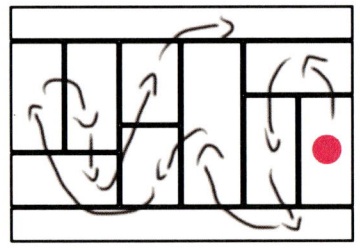
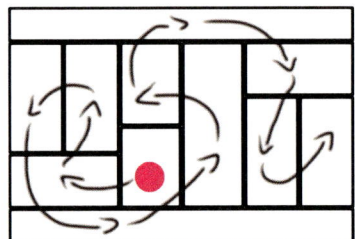

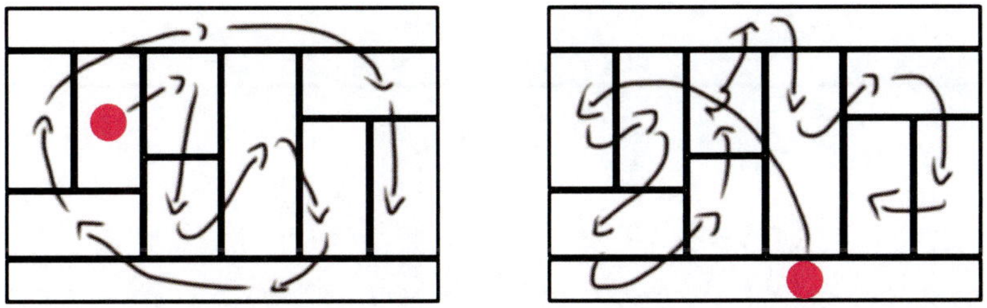

Which is **yours?**

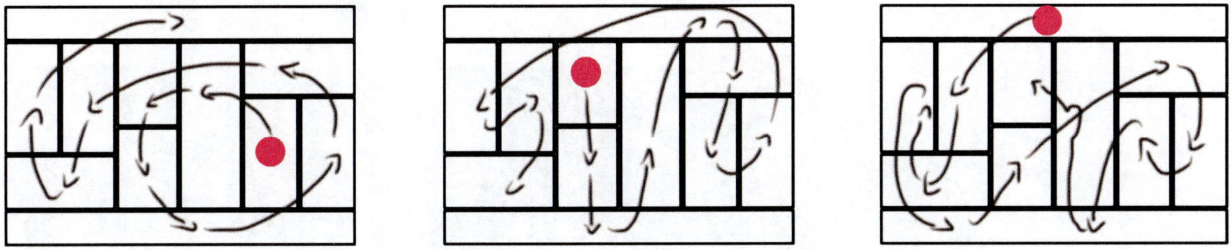

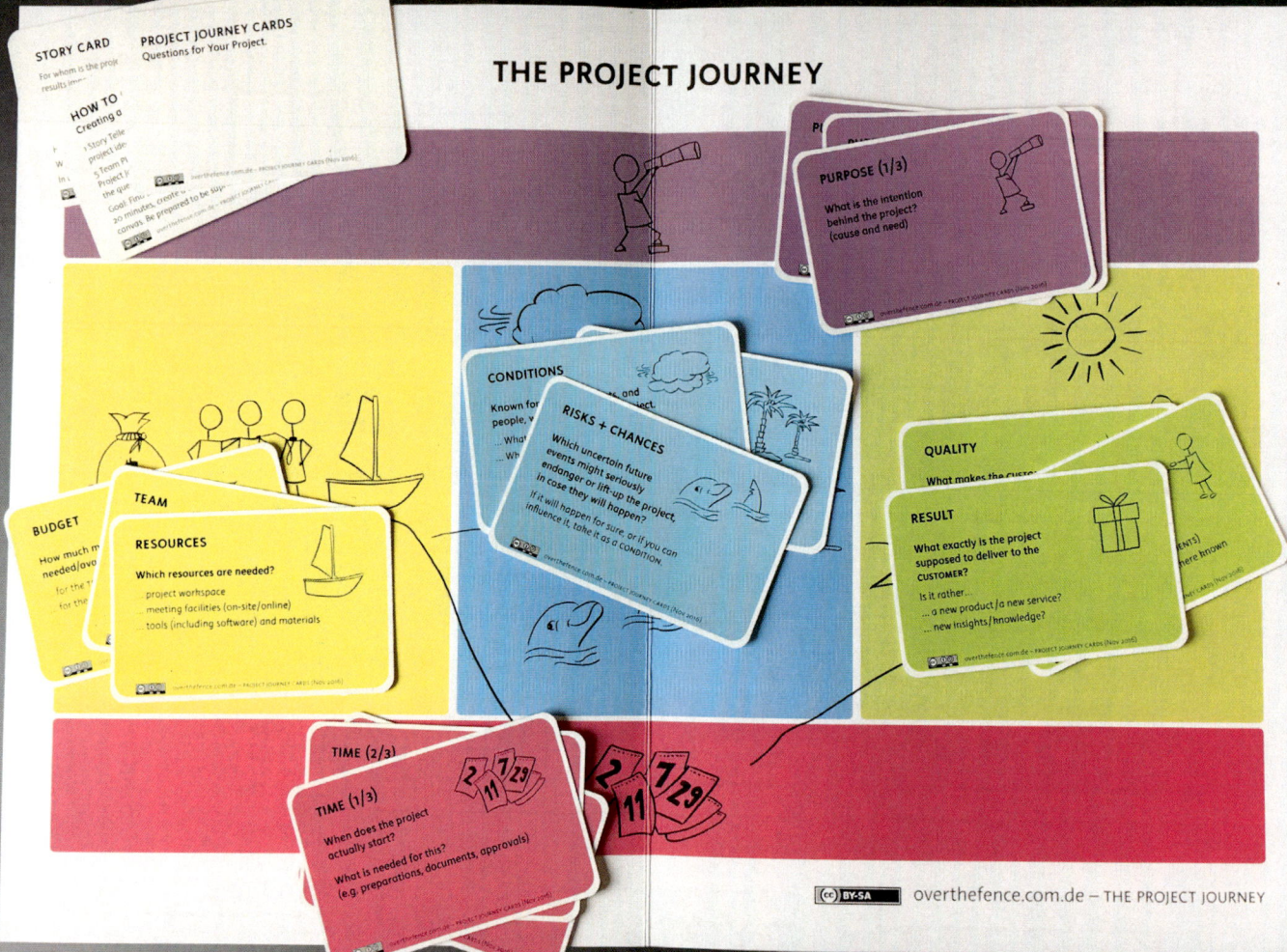

Experience the Project Journey

The project canvas provides 11 building blocks to describe your project. Principally, you can start designing your project with any building block – and proceed wherever you like. The project canvas will flexibly support your effort.

This flexibility is great news, if you are experienced in projects. However, if you are less experienced, many degrees of freedom can be confusing. In this case, you might possibly want some more guidance. This is why we have invented the Project Journey Experience.

The Project Journey Experience provides a good practice of how to develop an initial project design in less than two hours. This practice includes rules of communication as well as a recommended sequence for working through the project canvas. By applying the Project Journey Experience you benefit from the wisdom of great project managers and experienced workshop facilitators.

The Project Journey Experience requires a set of journey cards. You can either order the material via the "Over the Fence" website or create it on your own. For your convenience, the following pages provide templates for the journey cards.

If you would like to perform a Project Journey Experience, contact us. We would be happy to share handy tips of how to best organize and host such a workshop. We wish you magic conversations!

PROJECT JOURNEY CARDS
Questions for Your Project.

PURPOSE (2/3)

Why is the project meaningful and important – and for whom?

PURPOSE (3/3)

How will the project change the future – and for whom?

PURPOSE (1/3)

What is the intention behind the project?
(cause and need)

HOW TO GET STARTED
Creating a shared picture based on a story

1 Story Teller (case giver) introduces a current project or project idea using the Story Card in 5 minutes.

5 Team Players have the mission to discover all areas of the Project Journey. Each person focuses on one area guided by the questions cards.

Goal: Find as many answers as possible for your cards. After 20 minutes, create a common picture of the project on the canvas. Be prepared to be suprised!

 overthefence.com.de – PROJECT JOURNEY CARDS (Nov 2016)

STORY CARD

For whom is the project important – and why?
What do you want to achieve?
What is important for you?
When are the results needed?
How do you want to proceed?
What is the biggest challenge?
In which case would you celebrate?

 overthefence.com.de – PROJECT JOURNEY CARDS (Nov 2016)

RESULT

What exactly is the project supposed to deliver to the CUSTOMER?

Is it rather...
... a new product / a new service?
... new insights / knowledge?

 overthefence.com.de – PROJECT JOURNEY CARDS (Nov 2016)

QUALITY

What makes the CUSTOMER really happy regarding...

... the RESULT of the project?
... the MILESTONES of reaching the result?
... the way of being informed/involved during the project?

 overthefence.com.de – PROJECT JOURNEY CARDS (Nov 2016)

CUSTOMER

Who is actually the customer?

People who...
... pay for the project (SPONSOR)
... start & stop the project (OWNER)
... are impacted by the results (RECIPIENTS)

In case of multiple customers: are there known conflicts?

 overthefence.com.de – PROJECT JOURNEY CARDS (Nov 2016)

RISKS + CHANCES

Which uncertain future events might seriously endanger or lift-up the project, in case they will happen?

If it will happen for sure, or if you can influence it, take it as a CONDITION.

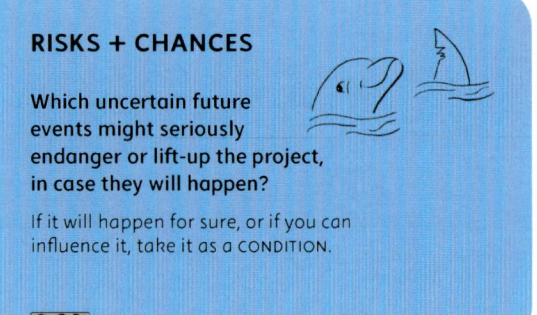

MILESTONES
MOMENTS TO CELEBRATE

What are important stages of progress?

Due dates for…
… intermediate results
… crucial decisions
… visible/measurable accomplishments

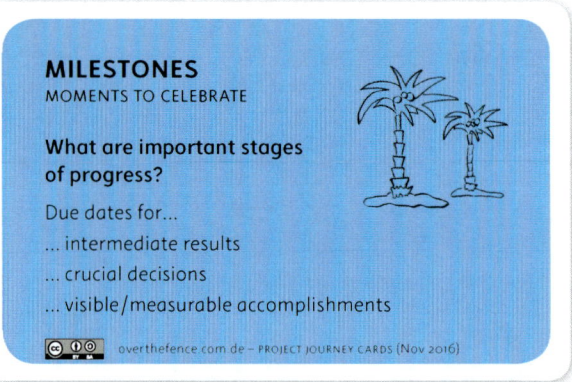

CONDITIONS

Known forces, facts, events, and people, which influence the project.

… What/who is supporting the project?
… What/who is hindering the project?

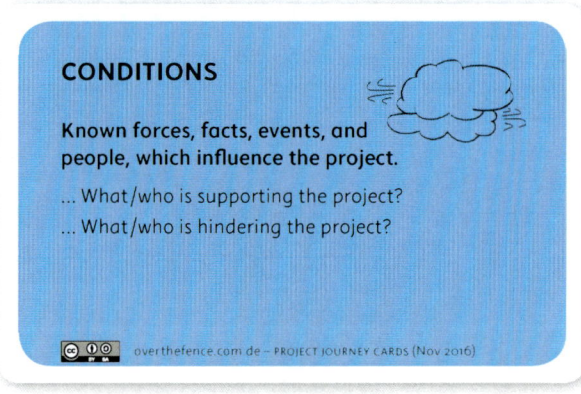

TEAM

Who is/should be on board?

… in the core team
… in the extended team
… as external partners
… as project leader/manager

RESOURCES

Which resources are needed?

… project workspace
… meeting facilities (on-site/online)
… tools (including software) and materials

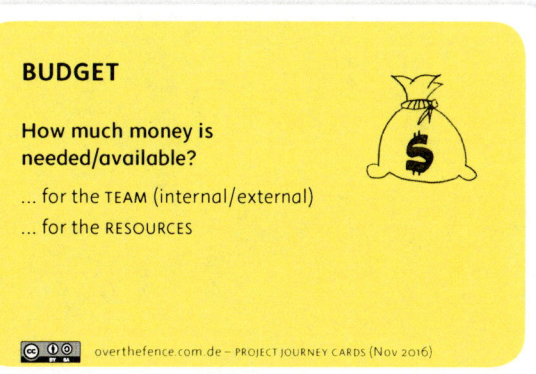

BUDGET

How much money is needed/available?

... for the TEAM (internal/external)
... for the RESOURCES

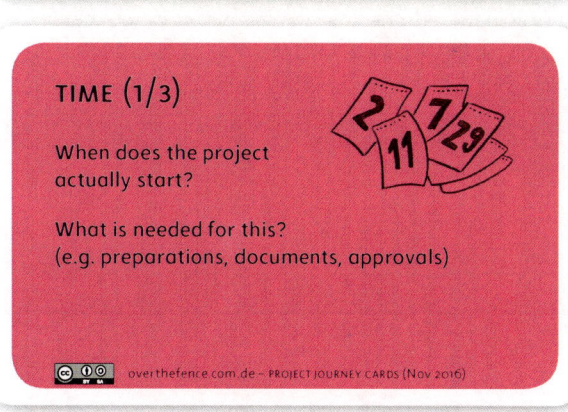

TIME (1/3)

When does the project actually start?

What is needed for this?
(e.g. preparations, documents, approvals)

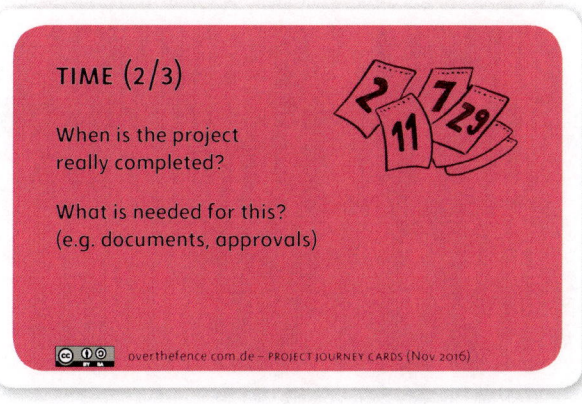

TIME (2/3)

When is the project really completed?

What is needed for this?
(e.g. documents, approvals)

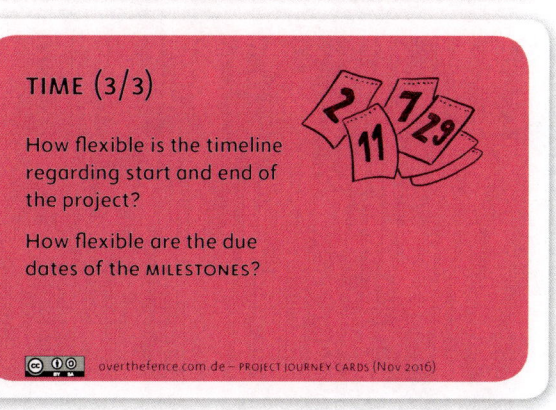

TIME (3/3)

How flexible is the timeline regarding start and end of the project?

How flexible are the due dates of the MILESTONES?

A Good Practice for Essential Project Design

1. Each great Project Journey Experience starts with the OWNER of the project. This person should participate in the workshop and tell the story of the project (see "story card").
2. From the owner's story, figure out the true PURPOSE of the project.
3. Next, define the RESULT of the project. What should the project create in order to meet the project purpose?
4. Who will receive the project result? The RECIPIENT can be identical with the owner or a different target person or group.
5. What is the latest DATE the project result should be handed over to the recipient?
6. Double-check: are owner, recipient, purpose, result and due date correct and well-orchestrated? If so, the OUTPUT of your project is essentially defined. Now, agree on a procedure to map out the remaining building blocks of the project canvas.

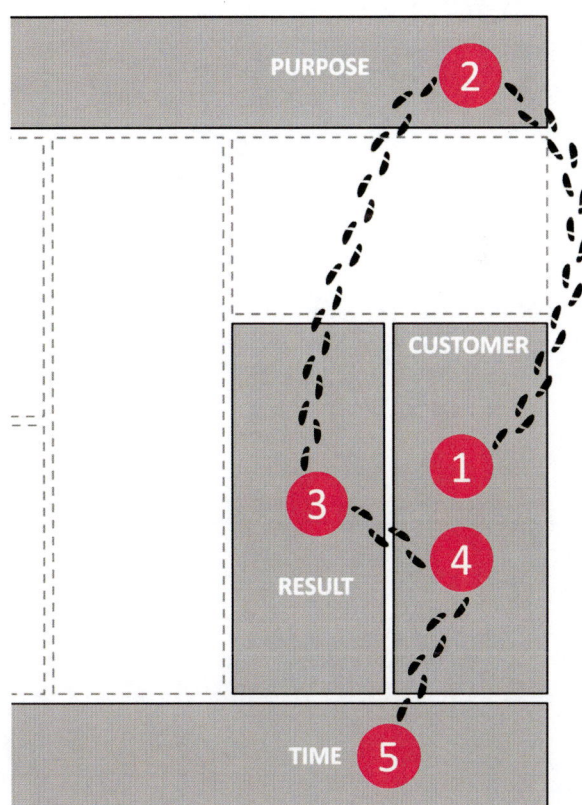

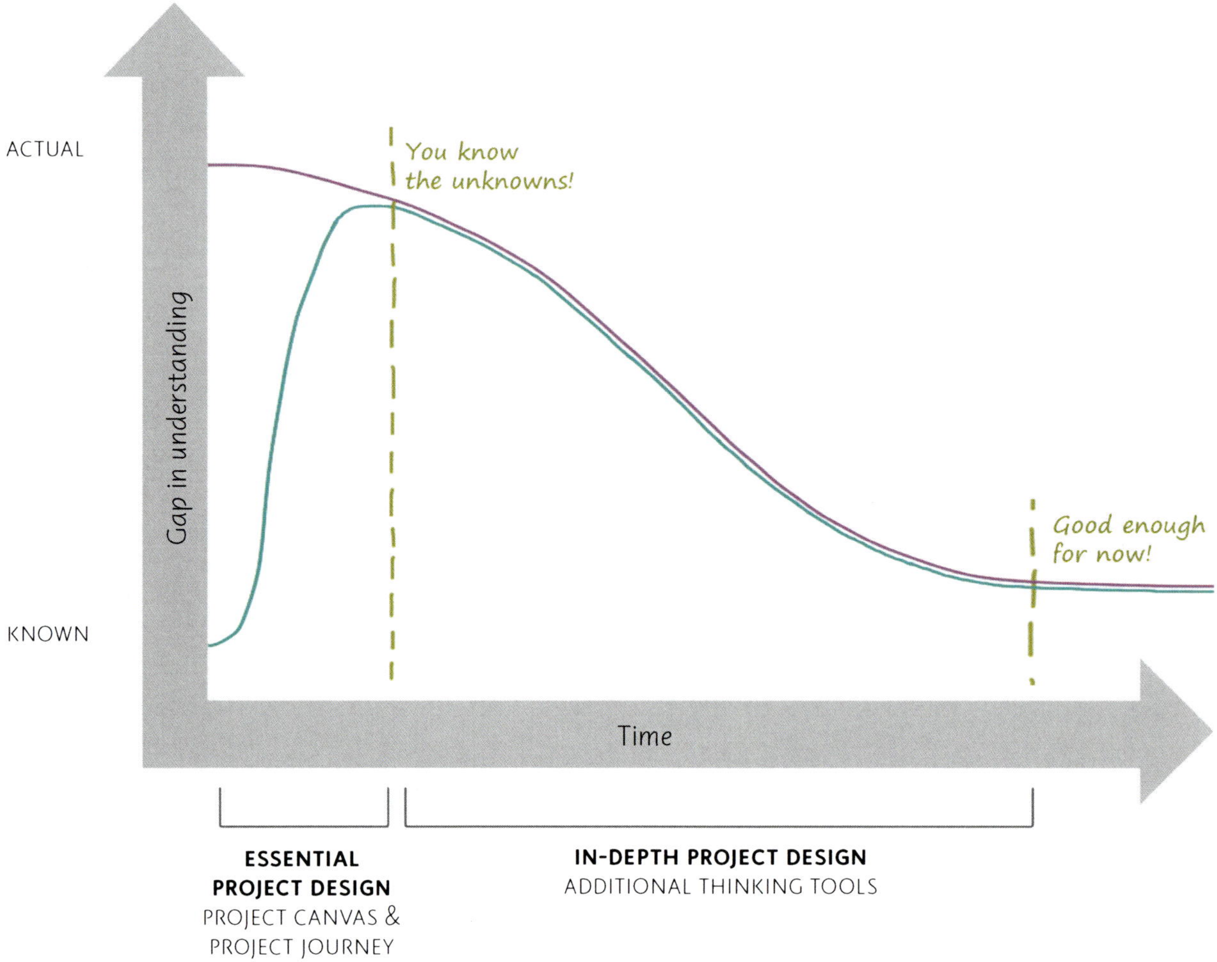

ACTUAL

Gap in understanding

You know the unknowns!

Good enough for now!

KNOWN

Time

ESSENTIAL PROJECT DESIGN
PROJECT CANVAS & PROJECT JOURNEY

IN-DEPTH PROJECT DESIGN
ADDITIONAL THINKING TOOLS

Magic Conversations (Part II)

A project team is a collection of people who have been put together for a unique endeavour. **One of the greatest traps in projects is the illusion, that people think alike.** Of course assuming this is always a problem, but in everday work we can learn to cope with it. Over weeks and months and years, we get used to our colleagues and figure out how they tick; we can experiment, practice, and eventually develop routines. In projects, we don't have this time!

Essential project design helps to quickly develop a common ground (see "Magic Conversations, Part I"). Beyond this, **essential project design helps to swiftly identify the known unknowns.**

When you initially apply the project canvas, you create a sketch of your project. This sketch offers two main benefits: (a) it is a common picture and (b) it reveals those parts of your project, which are in need of in-depth design.

While essential project design may be done in a few hours; in-depth design can take days or even weeks. This of course is only true for very complex projects. Less complex projects might already be completely designed after the "essential" procedure.

Essential project design comprises the initial canvas session – with or without the journey procedure. In-depth design applies additional thinking tools (see the following "design lessons").

However detailed you design your project; you will never be able to reach a complete understanding before the project. A certain amount of uncertainty is part of each project. Complete your project design, when it is "good enough for now" and the team feels prepared to start the venture.

"The greatest enemy of knowledge is not ignorance, it is the illusion of knowledge."

__ Stephen Hawking, theoretical physicist

IN-DEPTH

PROJECT DESIGN

Thinking Tools for Good Project Design

In the following chapter, we present 23 lessons for good project design. Each lesson describes how you can design one specific building block of your project (e.g. RESULT, TEAM, CUSTOMER, etc.). A few lessons however aim at shaping the links between the blocks.

Basically, the lessons help to map out the project canvas in-depth. For this, they provide visual "tools" as well as recommended "procedures" on how to use these tools.

The provided tools are no solution in itself – the solution is in you. The tools just help you consider crucial questions and smartly work out a good project design. Therefore, we call them "thinking tools".

Do I need to apply all tools?
Clearly, no. Just decide, which parts of your project are in need of in-depth design. If, for example, you feel that you should spend more time on the "customer" perspective, apply the related lessons 1 and 2. The table on the right shows, which lesson helps you to work out which building block of your project.

Can I change the procedure?
Clearly, yes. We have described the "procedures" of how to use the tools for people, who are not that experienced in organizing workshops and facilitating communication. If you are an experienced facilitator, feel free to develop your own procedure. We would love to hear about your experiences.

> "I work using the Brian Eno school of thinking: limit your tools, focus on one thing and just make it work... You become very inventive with the restrictions you give yourself."
>
> __ Anton Corbijn, photographer and film director

23 LESSONS FOR SHAPING THE 11 BUILDING BLOCKS OF ANY PROJECT

		CUSTOMER	PURPOSE	RESULT	QUALITY	BUDGET	TIME	MILESTONES	TEAM	RESOURCES	CONDITIONS	RISKS/CHANCES
1	GET TO KNOW YOUR CUSTOMER	X										
2	FIND OUT WHAT CUSTOMERS REALLY WANT	X										
3	UNDERSTAND THE PURPOSE OF YOUR PROJECT		X									
4	DETERMINE THE DESIRED RESULT			X	X							
5	BALANCE THE WHY WITH THE WHAT		X	X								
6	CRAFT A MEANINGFUL MISSION STORY		X	X								
7	AGREE ON THE PROJECT PROCEDURE				X							
8	SPECIFY CRUCIAL MILESTONES						X	X				
9	DEFINE THE MOMENT OF DONE				X			X				
10	BRING SUPERPOWERS TOGETHER								X			
11	EQUIP YOUR PROJECT WISELY									X		
12	ALWAYS KNOW YOUR TIME						X					
13	SCALE YOUR BUDGET					X						
14	SET THE RIGHT SCOPE				X	X	X					
15	SENSE THE ENVIRONMENT										X	
16	PUT YOURSELF IN YOUR STAKEHOLDERS' SHOES										X	
17	EXPLORE UNCERTAINTIES										X	X
18	BE AWARE OF RISKS AND CHANCES											X
19	SHAPE THE SCOPE, SHAPE IT, SHAPE IT				X	X	X					
20	PURSUE THE QUALITY PATH				X							
21	BE SMART							X				
22	ILLUMINATE BLIND SPOTS										X	
23	PUT IT ALL TOGETHER											
	frequency of building blocks treated	2	3	3	6	3	4	3	1	1	4	2

are your tools ...

agile?

If you ask, whether our tools support the ideals of the "agile manifesto", the answer is yes. If the question implies, whether they are specifically made for Scrum, the answer is no. For us, "agility" means a way of thinking, not a dogma. Therefore, the tools presented in this book can be combined with any project approach, agile as well as traditional.

novel?

Some of the presented tools are entirely new and invented by us. Others are "classics with a twist". The twist usually comes from combining a traditional project management technique with "design thinking", "improvisation", "gamification" or a combination thereof. This way, effectivity meets fun at work, yay!

helpful?

"A fool with a tool is still a fool." Ron Weinstein's famous sentence is often quoted when it comes to software tools and other gadgets. We believe that the statement is less true for "thinking tools". The tools in this book demonstrate, that nobody needs to be a "project fool". **Be yourself, be human, ask the right questions – and you will succeed.**

Thinking Tools for
PROJECT DESIGN

- PURPOSE AND OUTCOME
- CUSTOMER HATS
- SYMPATHY MAP
- 5 WHYS
- 5 WHATS
- WHY-WHAT-BALANCE
- MISSION STORY FINDER
- PROCEDURE AND INPUT
- PROCEDURE TRIAD
- MILESTONE MAKER
- GAME OF DONE
- SUPERHERO RACI
- 5-10-15 INDEX OF RESOURCES
- TIME PLANNER
- BUDGET CONSTRUCTOR
- GOALS AND ENVIRONMENT
- SCOPINATOR
- WIND OF CHANGE
- DREAM HEADLINES
- UNCERTAINTY MAP
- AGILE IPRA
- CLOSING TIME
- MISSION POSSIBLE
- USER STORY – UNWRAP YOUR PRESENT – DESIGN THE BOX
- BE SMART CHECKLIST
- SPEEDBOAT "C"
- THE DISNEY METHOD

ARE YOU FACING A NEW PROJECT? HERE ARE LESSONS FOR A GOOD **PROJECT DESIGN.** **GET TO KNOW YOUR CUSTOMERS.** FIND OUT WHAT THEY REALLY WANT. **UNDERSTAND THE PURPOSE OF YOUR PROJECT.** DETERMINE THE DESIRED RESULT. BALANCE THE WHY WITH THE WHAT. CRAFT A MEANINGFUL MISSION STORY. **AGREE ON THE PROCEDURE.** SPECIFY CRUCIAL MILESTONES. DEFINE THE MOMENTS OF DONE. **BRING SUPERPOWERS TOGETHER.** EQUIP YOUR PROJECT WISELY. ALWAYS KNOW YOUR TIME. SCALE YOUR BUDGET. **SET THE RIGHT SCOPE.** SENSE THE ENVIRONMENT. PUT YOURSELF IN YOUR STAKEHOLDERS SHOES. EXPLORE UNCERTAINTIES. BE AWARE OF RISKS AND OPPORTUNITIES. SHAPE THE SCOPE, SHAPE IT, SHAPE IT. PURSUE THE QUALITY PATH. BE SMART. ILLUMINATE BLIND SPOTS. AND PUT IT ALL TOGETHER. BUT MORE THAN ANYTHING ELSE: BE HUMAN, BE YOURSELF, AKS QUESTIONS, ENJOY COLLABORATION, AND YOU WILL BENEFIT FROM INTERDISCIPLINARY **WISDOM.**

Design Inspired by Rachael Beresh

LESSONS FOR A GOOD PROJECT DESIGN

#

1.	Get to know your customer	59
2.	Find out what customers really want	67
3.	Understand the purpose of your project	71
4.	Determine the desired result	75
5.	Balance the "why" with the "what"	79
6.	Craft a meaningful mission story	83

The 3 schools of project thinking — 86

7.	Agree on the project procedure	93
8.	Specify crucial milestones	97
9.	Define the moment of done	101
10.	Bring superpowers together	109
11.	Equip your project wisely	115
12.	Always know your time	119
13.	Scale your budget	123

The art of scoping — 126

14.	Set the right scope	131
15.	Sense the environment	135
16.	Put yourself in your stakeholders' shoes	139
17.	Explore uncertainties	143
18.	Be aware of risks and chances	147
19.	Shape the scope, shape it, shape it	153
20.	Pursue the quality path	157
21.	Be smart	165
22.	Illuminate blind spots	169
23.	Put it all together	173

UP FOR A QUICK FUN RIDDLE?
4 CUSTOMERS IN THE DESERT

Four project customers are kidnapped by aliens and have been buried up to their necks in the desert. They can only look in one direction and can not move. There is a wall between customer 1 and 2, which they cannot see through.

Since the aliens have brainwashed them, each customer has forgotten which hat they are wearing. All they remember is that two of them are wearing "sponsor" (s) hats and the other two are wearing "owner" (o) hats. That's all they know.

To avoid dying of thirst, one of them must let the chief alien know what type of hat he is wearing. The customers only get one attempt and aren't allowed to speak. If they get it wrong, everyone will die.

After 2 minutes, one customer calls out the type of his hat. It's correct! Question: which customer is it and how did he figure it out?

solution, p. 181

Project Canvas: CUSTOMER

GET TO KNOW YOUR CUSTOMER

LESSON 1

A project customer can fill different roles. Or, in other words, a customer can wear three "hats". The three roles are: **owner, sponsor,** and **recipient** (see the book "CANVAS" for further information). Each role implies a specific reponsibility and specific interests (which can be conflicting), understanding customer roles is vital for a successful project.

Each project is characterized by a particular customer constellation. For example, some projects only have one single customer (person), who is wearing all three "hats". In contrast, other projects have dozens of customers, involving multiple sponsors, owners, and recipients.

Since it is crucial to be familiar with your project's customers, this first lesson guides you to create a list of your customers and find out who is wearing which hat.

SHORTHAND
Identify the customers of your project and understand their different roles

DIFFICULTY
Medium

MAIN TECHNIQUE
Customer Hats

PARTICIPANTS
You (and project customers)

TIME
2 hours

"A lamp cannot play the role of the sun and the sun cannot play the role of a lamp."
__Amit Kalantri, author

CUSTOMER HATS

PURPOSE OF USE
To identify the customers of your project – and to clearly know their different roles: owner, sponsor, recipient.

PARTICIPANTS
You, customer(s)

TYPE OF MEETING
Individual reflection and/or workshop-like session plus customer interviews

DURATION
2 hours or more (based on the number of customers)

GEAR
Customer Hats worksheet

Tip: you can perform this initial reflection either alone (self-study) or in a joint brainstorming session with your project team (workshop).

PROCEDURE

1. Start with exploring the background and the history of your project. Ask yourself, who actually initiated the project, who has a demand for the results of the project, who invests money for it, and why? Create a list of the identified persons/groups.

2. Usually, it's not sufficient to "think on your own". To make sure that your list is complete and correct, interview the initially identified customers. In case of a group, identify a key person from this group. In a customer interview, ask the questions below (see box).

3. Once you have completed your interviews, organize your notes and close your list.

4. Visualize your result! Draw a column for each customer (i.e. person or group). Following this, draw a line for each role/hat. You will get a table similar to the one on the right. Now, mark who is wearing which hat.

5. What does your result look like? What does it mean for your project? Compare your "customer hats" with typical project constellations (see following pages).

Questions for identifying project customer(s) and their various roles:
– Who pays for the project? (Sponsor)
– Who invests financially in the project? (Sponsor)
– Who holds the project budget? (Sponsor)
– Who can start and stop the project? (Owner)
– Who will own the project result? (Owner)
– Who will finally approve the project result? (Owner)
– Who will apply the result of the project? (Recipient)
– Who will directly benefit from the result? (Recipient)
– Who else is impacted by the result? (Recipient)

CUSTOMER HATS

Who is wearing which hat?

	Customer 1 (person/group)	...	Customer n (person/group)
S Sponsor			
O Owner			
R Recipient			

CUSTOMER HATS

Sponsor — L.J. Green (Director Marketing)
Owner — L.J. Green (Director Marketing)
Recipient — L.J. Green (Director Marketing)

ONE PARTY

The simplest constellation is dealing with only one person. Which means, the party who pays for the project directly receives the result and benefits from its values.

Two examples for such projects are reviewing an existing product strategy and developing a market study (commissioned by the Director Marketing). In both cases, the result (i.e. a kind of written report) would be handed-over to the owner.

Sponsor — T.C. Spencer (COO)
Owner — T.C. Spencer (COO)
Recipient — People in Building B2 (245 persons who are located in Elmstr. 13b)

OWNER NOT RECIPIENT

In corporate practice, this is a very common constellation. Often, projects are commissioned by a kind of executive, but the positive effects should be generated on various other business levels.

One simple project example is moving to a new office building. In this case, the owner could be the "Chief Operational Officer (COO)" and the recipients, i.e. the target group, are all persons who have to move to the new building.

CUSTOMER HATS

	J.F. Lee (Founder)	M. Penny (Account Manager, Venture Money Ltd.)
S Sponsor		X
O Owner	X	
R Recipient	X	

	J.F. Lee (Founder)	The Crowd (1.047 micro investors)
S Sponsor		X
O Owner	X	
R Recipient	X	

OWNER NOT SPONSOR

Also commonly, sponsors and owners are different parties. Often, people have great ideas but lack the money to realize them. In such cases, a source of funding is needed. Sources of funding are e.g. banks, private persons/companies and public investors. An example project would be if e.g. a venture capital company provides money to an entrepreneur for developing an innovative business model.

Financial sponsors are not really interested in the project result (unless they are owners, too); they solely expect a financial return of their investment.

Crowd-funded projects are another example of the same scenario (i.e. the owner IS NOT the sponsor).

In crowd-funded projects, many people give smaller amounts of money to support a project, e.g. the invention of a new product. Through this, "the crowd" becomes the sponsor of the project (but not necessarily the owner).

CUSTOMER HATS

	J.F. Lee (Head of Human Resources, UK)	T. Klein (Chief Information Officer, UK)	M.L. Benn (Director Global Procurement)	HR Team (UK, 15 persons)	Advisors (Globally, 3,400 persons)	IT Team (UK, 4 persons)
S Sponsor			X			
O Owner	X	X				
R Recipient				X	X	X

* Original names have been replaced.

One of The Big 4

In corporate practice, things are often even more complicated. Particularly in big organizations, where structures are multi-dimensional and responsibilities are shared, projects have multiple customers.

For example, let's take the implementation of a major online learning program in a global audit and advisory company. In this case, the project had two owners, the Head of HR (the business owner) and the CIO (the technical owner). They both belong to the UK firm, that was running the project for the entire group. The project was funded by a central corporate budget, i.e. the sponsor was from Global Procurement. Last but not least, the project had three recipients. Firstly, people from UK's HR Team, who are in charge of providing business services along with the new system. Secondly, guys from UK's IT Team who are hosting and technically supporting the new solution. And thirdly, the globally spread advisors who are the actual target group of the learning program.

PROJECT COMES FROM PROJECTION

Project Canvas: CUSTOMER & PURPOSE

FIND OUT WHAT CUSTOMERS REALLY WANT

LESSON 2

The key people in your project are the project owners. Not only can they start and stop your project, they will eventually let you know whether your project is a success or not.

Once you truly understand the goals, interests, and beliefs of the project owner, your work will be much easier. And if you sympathize with the owner's goals as well, you are likely to have a great time in your project.

The "Sympathy Map" is a tool that helps to work out the project owner's personal goals, fears, and interests. In combination with a few powerful questions, this tool makes implicit assumptions explicit and thus reveals the true purpose of the project.

SHORTHAND
Interview the project owner(s) and find out their personal interests, pains and gains

DIFFICULTY
Medium to Hard

MAIN TECHNIQUE
Sympathy Map

PARTICIPANTS
Owner(s), Team

TIME
1,5 hours (per owner)

"The customer's perception is your reality."

__ Kate Zabriskie, instructional designer

SYMPATHY MAP

PURPOSE OF USE
To ultimately understand your project owner; to reveal potential conflicts of interests in case of multiple owners.

BACKGROUND
The SYMPATHY MAP is a modified "empathy map" which has originally been invented by the company XPLANE. This tool also includes a "pain gain map" which has been invented by Dave Gray for product and service design. We don't need every aspect of the original tool but focus on project specifics. Thus we adapted the empathy map and named it SYMPATHY MAP as a reminiscence.

PARTICIPANTS
Owner(s), and (potentially) team.

TYPE OF MEETING
Interview-like session (one per owner). In case of multiple owners, you need to conduct multiple interviews.

DURATION
1h per interview, plus 30 minutes for summarizing and organizing the Sympathy Map.

GEAR
Sympathy Map worksheet (see right), pens & sticky notes

SAY AND DO? OBSERVE the public behavior of the project owner; capture "official" explanations, stories, stated reasons, facts. How does the owner act in their (business) role, e.g. as Director of Sales or CEO?

THINK AND FEEL? INTERPRET your observations. Try to describe the mind-set of the project owner; figure out beliefs, thoughts, values, dreams, implicit assumptions. What do you conclude from the "SAY AND DO"? What truly moves this person; what truly matters? What is the personal (hidden) agenda?

PAIN What kind of problem, frustration, annoyance need be sorted out by the project? Which fears/concerns does the owner have, as to why the project might not work out?

GAIN Which result is desired; which value should be created; what does success look like for the owner?

PROCEDURE

1. Interview the owner. Use powerful questions (see below) to allow the owner dream and envision the future.

2. Observe shown behavior, write down given statements. Don't interpret, stick to obvious facts. Take notes on sticky notes.

3. Arrange the sticky notes on the Map in "SAY AND DO".

4. How can the SAY AND DO be interpreted? Consider (in your team) and fill in "THINK AND FEEL"

POWERFUL QUESTIONS
IMAGINE the project has been a great success ...

... what would you be particularly proud of?
... how would the world look differently – what would have changed?
... how would you like people to speak about the project?
... which value would have been created ... and for whom?
... which main problem would have been solved?

SYMPATHY MAP

PAIN **GAIN**

What does s_he think and feel?

emotions
beliefs
assumptions
perceptions
values
etc.

What does s_he say and do?

actions
statements
explanations
instructions
comments

PAIN **GAIN**

LESSONS

Over the Fence
WHY KIDS ASK WHY

Why is the sky blue? Why can bees fly? Why do I have to be nice? A child's never-ending "whys" are genuine approaches to understanding the world, scientists say.

Fifty years ago, research stated that kids under 7 years of age couldn't differentiate between cause and effect. More recent studies revealed that kids get causality much earlier. As early as the age of 3, kids repeat their initial "why" question, if they don't get a response – they follow-up up with in-depth "whys" until the answer is satisfying.

Kids are interested in causality and an optimal level of information. This is what we can learn from toddlers.

Project Canvas: PURPOSE

DEFINE THE PURPOSE OF YOUR PROJECT

LESSON 3

Why is your project needed – why is it meaningful and important? And for whom? The purpose of a project – just like any purpose in life – serves as a guiding principle. A guiding principle must be genuine, precise, and easy to understand. This is what we expect from a well-defined project purpose.

Defining the purpose of your project means analyzing the history and the background of your venture. It leads to the origins of your project, the hidden agendas as well as the official agendas.

The persons who can inform you about the project purpose are the project owners. They made the decision to initiate the project and therefore know the true cause(s) of the project.

Be aware that in case of multiple project owners (see lesson 1), people might have different views regarding the purpose of a project. Arrange sufficient time for developing a common gound.

SHORTHAND
Meet project owners and discover why this project is actually needed (valuable and important).

DIFFICULTY
Simple to Medium

MAIN TECHNIQUE
5 Whys

PARTICIPANTS
Project Owner(s)

TIME
approx. 60 minutes

Tip: The "5 Whys" technique can also be used in combination with the "Sympathy Map" and powerful questions (see lesson 2).

"He who has a WHY to live for can bear almost any how."
__ Friedrich Nietzsche, philosopher

5 WHYS

PURPOSE OF USE
To define a meaningful project purpose; to reveal the actual need of the project.

BACKGROUND
Invented by Sakichi Toyoda (and applied at Toyota Motor Corporation), the original method aims at revealing the root cause of a (technical) defect or problem. In a broader sense, 5 Whys can be understood as an iterative question-asking-technique to explore the underlying cause-and-effect relationships of anything.

PARTICIPANTS
You and owner(s)

TYPE OF MEETING
Workshop-like session. In case of multiple owners, invite all owners to the same session.

DURATION
60 minutes or less

GEAR
Pens & sticky notes, whiteboard

PROCEDURE

1. Prepare a whiteboard. Write down the question "Why do we need the project?" (name the project). Draw 5 lines, all starting with "WHY?". Draw one column per owner.

2. Prepare sticky notes: Distribute five of them per owner, numbered from 1 to 5.

3. Invite the owners to answer the question on the whiteboard and write down their response on sticky note #1.

4. Referring to their response on the sticky note, ask the owners, "Why is this important or valuable?" Let them note the reponse on the subsequent sticky note.

5. Repeat until all sticky notes are filled.

6. Arrange the sticky notes on the whiteboard: per owner in numeric order.

7. In case of multiple owners: review and discuss until a consensus is reached.

WHY
IS IT
MEANINGFUL, VALUABLE, IMPORTANT?

Tip: In case of multiple owners, 5 Whys will reveal their different professional perspectives and preceptions (see example on the right page).

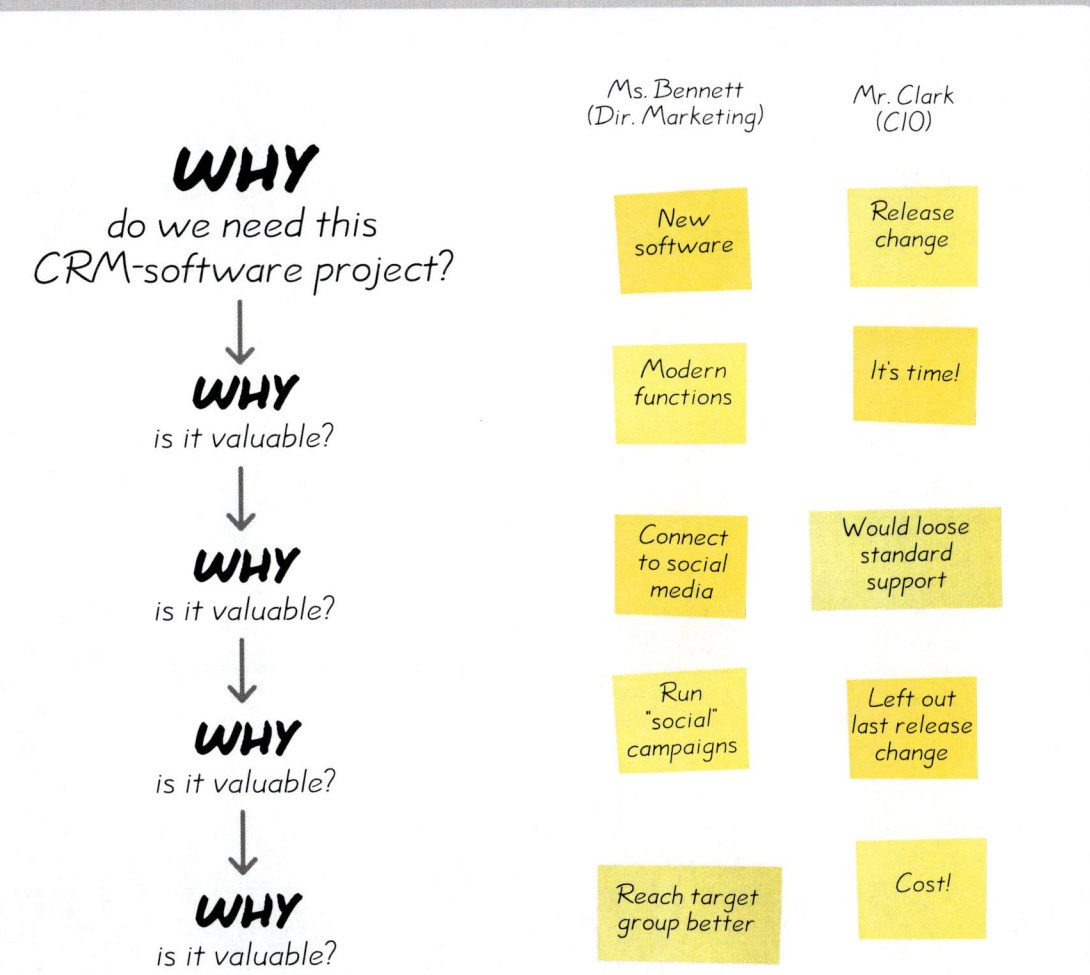

WE MUST ALL FACE THE CHOICE BETWEEN WHAT IS RIGHT AND WHAT IS EASY

__ Albus Dumbledore

Project Canvas: RESULT & QUALITY (of result)

DETERMINE THE DESIRED RESULT

LESSON 4

The project RESULT is the "output" of your project. It's WHAT your project creates, produces or builds and what you eventually hand over to the customer.

Each project results in either a physical PRODUCT, a SERVICE, or new KNOWLEDGE (or a combination thereof). These are the main three types of results — each demanding a special type of expertise for creating it.

A project result can be described by it's "form and function" and deconstructed into it's "pieces and parts". These characteristics and features determine the quality of a project result.

This lessons provides you with "5 Whats", an easy-to-use technique for clarifying your project's main result and it's main quality criteria.

SHORTHAND
Clarify the main result of your project

DIFFICULTY
Simple to Medium

MAIN TECHNIQUE
5 Whats

PARTICIPANTS
Project Owner(s)

TIME
45 minutes

"Can we build it? Yes we can!"

__ Bob the Builder, builder

5 WHATS

PURPOSE OF USE

To define the main result of the project, incl. it's core components. To define what artifact (or service/knowledge) the project creates.

PARTICIPANTS

You and owner(s)

TYPE OF MEETING

Workshop-like session. In case of multiple owners, invite all owners to the same session.

DURATION

45 minutes

GEAR

Pens & sticky notes, whiteboard

> Tip: Use 5 Whats before or after 5 Whys. If you start with 5 Whats, you can change the initial question in 5 Whys to "WHY SOULD THE PROJECT PRODUCE [Result xyz]?"

PROCEDURE

1. Prepare a whiteboard. Write down the question "What should the project produce?" (to reach the purpose). Make 5 lines, all starting with "WHAT?". Create one column per owner.

2. Prepare the following four question cards:
(i) What is it exactly?
(ii) What are it's main components?
(iii) What else should be created?
(iv) What should be delivered to the customer at the end of the project?

3. Prepare sticky notes: Distribute five of them per participant, numbered 1 through 5.

4. Invite the participants to answer the question on the whiteboard and write down their response to sticky note #1.

5. Follow-up with the question on question card (i) and repeat for all questions.

6. Arrange the sticky notes on the whiteboard: per project owner per question card (i.e. as a table).

7. In case of multiple owners: review and discuss until a consensus is reached.

> 5 Whats can also be applied within a diverse project team to create a shared understanding among different professional experts.

Up for a quick exercise?
WHAT MAKES A GREAT PAIR?

RESULT
What does the project produce?
(tangible and qualifiable output:
Product, Service, Knowledge)

PURPOSE
Why does the project exist?
(specific meaningful need;
desired valuable effect)

NEW SALES STRATEGY

MAKE PROFIT

Re-designed
CORPORATE WEBSITE

Improve
CORPORATE WEBSITE

FEASIBILITY STUDY
E-Mobility 3.0

Provide our customers
with **E-MOBILITY EXPERIENCE**

Re-organized
OFFICE SPACE

Stimulate informal
COMMUNICATION

Above, you see four pairs of result and purpose. These examples have been taken from real projects. Only one pair is "great". This pair describes a clear result, a meaningful purpose and a good balance between result and purpose. The other three pairs have an issue in either result, purpose or balance. Can you find out which pair is best (and why)?

solution, p. 182

Project Canvas: PURPOSE & RESULT

BALANCE THE "WHY" WITH THE "WHAT"

LESSON 5

Each project addresses a certain need. This need determines the purpose of the project. And each project produces a specific result in order to satisfy this need. In other words, the result is the means to reach the project purpose. **The RESULT is "what" the project creates; the PURPOSE is "why" it is created.** Aligning the "Why" with the "What" includes three crucial aspects:

1. A meaningful "Why" that goes beyond the pure existence of the result (what is the actual value of the result, what is the desired effect?).

2. The best "What" for a given "Why". Typically, there are multiple options to reach a purpose. Which is best?

3. The right sizes of "What" and "Why". If your "What" is too small, it will not be sufficient to reach the "Why". If the "Why" is too big, it won't be manageable within a single project.

Aligning project purpose and result can be quite tricky. Alternatingly asking "Why" and "What" helps you cope with it.

SHORTHAND
Find the best combination of project output (result) and desired effect (purpose)

DIFFICULTY
Hard

MAIN TECHNIQUE
Why-What Balance

PARTICIPANTS
Owner, Team

TIME
60 minutes

"I have no special talents, I am only passionately curious."

__ Albert Einstein, theoretical physicist

WHY-WHAT BALANCE

PURPOSE OF USE

To define a result that suits the purpose (and vice versa); to understand the pieces and parts of the result as well as their meaning for reaching the purpose; to ultimately align the project purpose (Why) with the project result (What).

PARTICIPANTS

Team and owner(s)

TYPE OF MEETING

Workshop-like session. In case of multiple owners, invite all owners to the same session.

DURATION

60 minutes

GEAR

Pens & sticky notes, whiteboard

PROCEDURE

1. Prepare a whiteboard by vertically dividing it. Label the left side result, and the right side purpose (see example on the right page). Distribute a sufficient amount of sticky notes as well as pens to the participants.

2. Under result, write down the desired project result. (Alternatively you could start with purpose).

3. Ask the participants, "Why do we need this?" Invite the participants to write down their responses on sticky notes.

4. Collect the responses, briefly discuss them and find a reasonable compromise (<3 minutes). Add it to the board under purpose.

5. Now ask, "What is needed for this (in detail)?" Invite the participants to write down their responses on sticky notes.

6. Collect the responses, allow a brief discussion, find a compromise (if needed), and write it down under result.

7. Repeat until all aspects are explored, and WHY and WHAT are accurate and well-orchestrated.

WHY DO WE NEED THIS?

WHAT DO WE NEED FOR THIS?

Tip: The "Why-What Balance" is best applied after 5 Whys (lesson 3) and 5 Whats (lesson 4), because after this you already have a solid understanding of project result and purpose. However, you can also use the "Why-What Balance" without having spent too much time on project result and purpose before. In this case, you should run several repetitions of the Why-What-Balance, alternately starting with result and purpose.

WHY-WHAT BALANCE

Result | **Purpose**

Market Study Japan

WHY do we need this? → Understand the Japanese market

WHAT do we need for this (in detail)? ← Data regarding competitors; buyers, products, etc.

WHY → Learn about sales channels, selling propositions, etc.

WHAT ← Analyze existing data sources; conduct own research

WHY → Prepare a sound decision pro/con market entry

WHAT ← A concise document, well-structured, with clear arguments (pro/con)

WHY → Support decision-making by our managing board

LESSONS

IT'S NOT ABOUT A VISION. IT'S ABOUT MAKING A VISION COME TRUE.

Project Canvas: PURPOSE & RESULT & CUSTOMER

CRAFT A MEANINGFUL MISSION STORY

LESSON 6

The mission story explains why your project exists. It's a statement of "what and why" – it states the purpose and the result of your project.

Each project has a mission and a vision. While mission means "action"; vision means "emotion". The vision is "the desire" of how the world should look after the project. The vision will be reached by an accomplished mission – your project!

A good mission story defines the object of your project in 15 seconds or less. This is written in a concise paragraph full of meaning. Choose your words carefully, refrain from using buzzwords, be very clear, and highlight the core value of your project.

Only a shared mission statement is a great mission statement! A statement, that is shared by the project owner(s) and team members becomes a powerful instrument of communication. Crafting a meaningful mission statement is quite simple, if you know the basic structure.

SHORTHAND
Describe the object of your project in 15 seconds

DIFFICULTY
Simple (if you have carried out the previous lessons)

MAIN TECHNIQUE
Mission Story Finder

PARTICIPANTS
Owner(s), Team

TIME
60 minutes

> "Good morning, Mr. Hunt. Your mission, should you choose to accept it, is (...)"
> __ Mission Commander Swanbeck, Mission Imposible II

MISSION STORY FINDER

A meaningful mission story has 3 core elements

1. The ACTION
2. The BENEFIT for the RECIPIENT
3. The BENEFIT for the OWNER

YOU CAN THINK OF EACH ELEMENT AS A SENTENCE IN YOUR MISSION STATEMENT.

The 1st sentence describes „what" the project will actually create. This addresses the project result (what will the project produce; which product, service or knowledge will be created)?

The 2nd sentence describes the value for the recipient. It explains how the recipient will benefit from the project result. It describes the positive impact the result will have for the target person or target group.

The 3rd sentence does the same for the project owner. It explains "why" the project was initiated. If owner and recipient are identical, you may not need to write this third sentence. If you have multiple owners, you might need one or two additional sentences to address the various values for the different owners.

MISSION STORY FINDER

Sometimes it helps to look at examples from actual projects. Here are three of them.

CORPORATE LEARNING
GLOBAL AUDIT AND ADVISORY FIRM

The mission of the project is to implement a corporate online learning system. The system will provide on-demand learning to each advisor in our wide-spread organization independent of location and language. As a result of the project, "Human Resources" will be able to conveniently track learning records of advisors and flexibly report to national legal authorities. This way the project will help our global firm to meet compliancy regulations.

SOFTWARE INNOVATION
UNIVERSITY RESEARCH INSTITUTE

The mission of the project is to invent a "Health & Fitness App for Project Managers". The project will create software-based services that could have positive effects on the health of any project manager. Particularly the risk of mental and physical breakdowns ("Burnout") will be reduced. Employers will benefit through higher performance and reduced times absent. The project supports the Digital Agenda of the Federal Ministry of Research.

OFFICE RELOCATION
PRODUCT AND SERVICE INNOVATION COMPANY

The mission of the project is to move the design department which is currently located in building B2 to our corporate headquarters. The project provides an open office environment with high-end technology and ergonomically friendly workplaces to all designers. The project brings designers closer to engineers and allows them to work shoulder-to-shoulder. This way, the project helps to foster informal communication and interdisciplinary collaboration.

LESSONS

MENTAL SIDE TRIP   **THE 3 SCHOOLS OF PROJECT THINKING**

The first six design lessons are meant for shaping the "output" of your venture. If you know what you want to get out of your project, it's time to think about a great way of creating it.

So, what are good practices for structuring a project? What are helpful steps and stages? What is a recommended procedure? In theory and practice, basically 3 different project approaches exist:

– **Traditional**
– **Prototypical**
– **Agile**

Project professionals call these the "procedural models of project management".

If you are experienced in projects, you may skip the following explanations or simply enjoy the story. If you are new to projects, the next paragraphs illuminate the fundamental options for organizing and structuring a project.

You will learn that there is no "best" procedure; simply there are three different schools of "project thinking", which are appropriate for various scenarios. Once you have understood the three schools of project thinking, you can even combine and blend elements of the approaches, if this appears to be beneficial.

And here the story goes ...

There were 3 kids,
William the oldest, and his two sisters, Paula and Amy. The three lived happily together with their parents, Mary and Marc. Marc was an engineer by heart, and Mary – not less passionate and skilled – a successful sculptor.

The three kids, even though they had the same parents (no milkman involved here), could not have been any different.

WILLIAM WORKS LIKE A WATERFALL...

They had their individual perceptions, mindsets, and talents. Nevertheless, all three were able to manage the challenges of life – with their diverse approaches.

First, let's talk about William. One sunny day, William had an idea. **"I want to build a swing"**, he stated aloud to himself. "But how?", he added less audibly.

William, entirely his father's son, immediately started to thoroughly analyze the challenge. What would the perfect swing look like?

The perfect swing would be designed for all three kids, it would be easy to assemble, independent of location, robust, weatherproof, and much more. William created a detailed list of requirements. His final list was comprised of dozens of requirements.

After having completed this analysis, William started his conceptual work. He made technical drawings and undertook concurrent mathematical calculations.

William was intensively thinking, drawing, calculating – producing a series of sophisticated models and elaborated plans. For these complicated tasks, he disappeared into his room, locked the door, and spent hours and hours in complete isolation.

MENTAL SIDE TRIP

PAULA LOVES PROTOTYPES...

On the other side of the door, his two sisters were wondering what William was doing.

But since they knew their older brother, they were not too worried, and went out into the garden to play.

When they got there, Paula had an idea. "I'll build a swing", she said to her little sister. And Amy smiled in joyful anticipation.

So Paula, entirely her mother's daughter, collected anything she could find. Loose tree branches, rusty screws, cardboard, rope, anything that was not nailed down, she worked into her first sample of a swing. Of course, this was premature in every respect. But it was suitable for demonstrating the idea and receiving Amy's response. Based on this response, Paula shaped the construction.

Paula re-built, showed the result, and Amy responded. This is how it went, until Amy was fairly happy with Paula's prototype.

Coincidentally, at that exact moment, William opened the door to his room and stated to have a great solution, too.

Now, the three could decide which concept they preferred to implement: William's theoretical model or Paula's physical prototype.

AND AMY IS AGILE.

Let's recap the situation.

William is a theoretician and analytical thinker. He plans like a waterfall. One plan flows into a more detailed plan until it eventually flows into the ultimate plan (or model), suitable for producing the desired result. William believes in a "best solution".

Paula in contrast is more of a pragmatic explorer. She does not believe in an objectively "best solution". For her, "best" is something that is designed for the needs of the customer. Figuring out these needs is Paula's ultimative challenge. And exploration is her approach to master this challenge. Paula's instruments for exploration are physical prototypes – they allow Paula to study customer reactions, first-hand and unfiltered.

Independent of these differences, William and Paula have similarities, too. Both aim at creating a "good model", that serves as a blueprint for the final result (output). The assumptions of what makes a model "good", are different, of course. But in the end, both approaches, (William's) Waterfall as well as (Paula's) Prototyping, have a long period of shaping the requirements before eventually producing the defined result.

And what about Amy?

As the youngest sister, she learned from the others.

From William she learned to plan. And from Paula she learned to show and adapt.

But Amy neither aims to create an ultimate plan, nor does she develop prototypes. Instead, Amy quickly produces useable results. Quite naturally, these results are comparably small, but they are fully functioning. And they can be used to build up a bigger product. This way, Amy invented something new, a step-by-step production. This procedure, she called the "agile" approach.

MENTAL SIDE TRIP (SUMMARY) — THE 3 SCHOOLS OF PROJECT THINKING

William loves the **waterfall**	Paula loves the **prototype**	Amy is **agile**

Plan	Create sample	Plan
Plan	Show	**Build small thing**
Plan	Create sample	Show
Plan	Show	...
...	...	Plan
Build everything	**Build everything**	**Build small thing**
Show	Show	Show

TRADITIONAL, PROTOTYPICAL, AGILE

	TRADITIONAL (e.g. Waterfall) Plan Plan Plan Plan ... **Build everything** Show	**PROTOTYPICAL** (e.g. Spiral) Create sample Show Create sample Show ... **Build everything** Show	**AGILE** (e.g. Scrum) Plan **Build small thing** Show ... Plan **Build small thing** Show
School of Thinking	Engineering	Exploring (trial-error)	Narrowing (step-by-step)
Character of Milestones	Documents	Prototypes	Partial results
Name of Project Stage	Phase	Loop	Sprint
Customer Contact Points	Rare (start/end)	Frequent (each loop)	Frequent (each sprint)
Change of Requirements	Not allowed (change request!)	Allowed (each loop)	Allowed (each sprint)

MENTAL SIDE TRIP

WHAT MAKES A GREAT PROJECT PROCEDURE?

for the **TEAM**

 for the **CUSTOMER**

for the **RESULT**

Project Canvas: QUALITY (of procedure)

AGREE ON A PROJECT PROCEDURE

LESSON 7

A project is a process! It has a clear starting point as well as a clear ending point. It serves a customer by transforming valuable input into a higher-valuable output.

The big question is: how to structure a project (process), so that it becomes efficient and effective? For this, there are three major approaches (aka "procedural models"):

    Traditional
    Prototypical
    Agile

If you are not familar with these "schools of project thinking", we recommend reading the previous six pages, before proceeding. None of the 3 procedural models is best per se. Whether an approach is advantageous, depends on the characteristics of your particular project.

As a rule of thumb, the selected procedure is great for your project, if it ...
(1) makes the customer happy
(2) makes the team happy
(3) fits the nature of the result

SHORTHAND
Understand the demands of the team, the customer, and the result and agree on an advantageous project procedure to meet these demands.

DIFFICULTY
Medium to Hard

MAIN TECHNIQUE
Procedure Triad

PARTICIPANTS
Owner, Recipient(s), Team

TIME
2 hours or more

> "Fall in love with the process, and the results will come."
> __ Eric Thomas, motivational speaker

PROCEDURE TRIAD

PURPOSE OF USE
To figure out the demands as well as the constraints of customer, team, and result. These are the boundary conditions for a "good project procedure".

PARTICIPANTS
Customer (owner, recipient), and core team

TYPE OF MEETING
Workshop-like session. Invite the core team, project owner(s) as well as representatives from the target group (recipients) to the same session.

DURATION
2 hours or more (depending on the complexity of the project)

GEAR
Pens & sticky notes, Procedure Triad worksheet (see page 92), prepared flip charts (or similar) with questions, addressing the customer, the team, and the result (see next page)

PROCEDURE

1. Put a large-size Procedure Triad worksheet on a wall. Prepare 3 flip charts with questions regarding the customer, the team, and the result (see next page). Distribute sufficient pens and sticky notes to the participants.

2. Start with CUSTOMER. Invite all the customers present to answer the questions on the flip chart "For the Customer" and write down their responses to sticky notes.

3. Now, instruct the TEAM in the same way: Invite the team to answer the questions on the flip chart "For the Team". Ask them to note their responses on sticky notes.

4. Allow 10 minutes (or more) for both groups. Stop them at the same time.

5. Invite the customers to put their sticky notes on the Triad worksheet (under the "For the Customer" section). Ask them to explain their answers to all participants. Allow clarifications.

6. Once completed, invite the team to perform the same exercise (putting their sticky notes under the "For the Team" section). Again, allow clarifications.

7. For an intermediate finding, compare the demands of both parties (customer vs. team). In case of conflicts, review and discuss until a consensus is reached.

8. Follow-up with RESULT. Ask all participants to answer the questions on the "For the Result" chart. Let them write down their responses on sticky notes.

9. Let the participants put their sticky notes on the worksheet (under the "For the Result" section). Invite everybody to study the notes of the others and group similar answers together.

10. Once all sticky notes are arranged, invite the participants to review and discuss the collected demands/contraints as well as their consequences for the project procedure. If a consensus is reached, confirm the key findings.

PROCEDURE TRIAD

What makes a great project procedure?

QUESTIONS

for the team

- Have you worked together as a team before?
- Do you prefer working side by side or as a distributed team?
- Which types of team meetings do you need; when/how often?
- How would you like to collaborate with the customer; in which situations and for which decisions do you need the customer?

for the customer

- How would you like to be involved/informed about the progress of the project?
- Would you like to have regular meetings; when/how often?
- How would you like to receive and approve results?
- What is your availability for project matters?
- Would you be available for any ad hoc appointments?

for the result

- How well do you know this type of project (a project for creating this type of result)?
- What are proven procedures for...
  ... conceptualizing
  ... producing
  ... releasing
  such a result?
- Are the requirements for the result well-known (specified) and stable (robust)?

Tip: Based on the type of the result, we can differentiate between PRODUCT projects, SERVICE projects, and KNOWLEDGE projects. Each type of result requires a subject-matter-specific procedure. (Read more in the CANVAS book/chapter "Result".)

Up for a quick exercise?
WHAT ARE THE MILESTONES?

THE WEDDING CAKE PROJECT

Imagine your best friend is getting married. As a present you plan to produce the best wedding cake ever. The cake should have 3 layers and some awesome features like chocolate roses, cream decoration and an icing, which displays the happy bridal couple.

What could be the milestones of your cake project? (Tip: The next pages provide some useful hints.)

solution, p. 183

Project Canvas: MILESTONES, TIME

SPECIFY CRUCIAL MILESTONES

LESSON 8

I remember milestones from childhood when I was "forced" to go on hiking trips with my grand-parents. These trips seemed to be as endless as eventless. Except for small stones, which appeared regularly by the roadside. Figures on the stones marked our progress. Therefore, passing a milestone was a very special moment – a moment of excitment and celebration.

The same is true for project milestones. A milestone in a project is a measurable goal. It structures the challenge and gives orientation.

Reaching a milestone typically means providing a "key deliverable" to the customer. This is a true reason to celebrate. Therefore, you should not forget to party a bit!

Project milestones are often defined iteratively – on various levels of detail. This lesson introduces the "Milestone Maker", an effective technique for taking the first step. Based on this first step, more detailed "criteria of done" can be specified quite easily.

SHORTHAND
Identify "key deliverables" and define related milestones of your project.

DIFFICULTY
Medium

MAIN TECHNIQUE
Milestone Maker

PARTICIPANTS
Customer, Team

TIME
60 minutes

"Things do not happen. Things are made to happen."

__ John F. Kennedy, 35th President of the United States

MILESTONE MAKER

PURPOSE OF USE
To identify key deliverables and determine their due dates (a milestone is a targeted key deliverable).

PARTICIPANTS
Customer (owner, recipient), and core team

TYPE OF MEETING
Workshop-like session. Invite the core team, project owner(s) as well as representatives from the target group (recipients) to the same session.

DURATION
1 hour or more (depending on the project complexity)

GEAR
Milestone Maker worksheet (recreated on the whiteboard), pens & sticky notes.

> Tip: The preferred type of milestone reveals the school of project thinking. In AGILE projects, milestones are "partial results" (ready to be put to use). In TRADITIONAL projects milestones are mostly plans, concepts, and a whole series (a "waterfall") of documents. And in PROTOYPING, milestones are – no surprise – prototypes.

PROCEDURE

1. Prepare a whiteboard by vertically dividing it. Label the left side DELIVERABLES, and the right side MILESTONES (see example on the right page). Distribute a sufficient amount of sticky notes as well as pens to the participants.

2. Start with DELIVERABLES. Divide this part of the board horizontally. Label the upper part PAPER and the lower part OTHER (see example). Explain that PAPER relates to all deliverables, which can be printed out (such as reports, plans, and all sorts of documents) while OTHER relates to the rest, e.g. physical products, innovation, etc.

3. Begin with PAPER. Invite the participants to name major deliverables in this regard. For example, ask whether particular management documents are required (such as reports, plans, etc.). Ask the participants to note their responses on sticky notes.

4. Proceed with the OTHER deliverables. Again, invite the participants to name respective deliverables. Ask the participants whether the delivery of "partial results" (components of the main result), is desired. Invite the participants to write down their reponses on sticky notes.

5. Let the participants put their sticky notes on the whiteboard. Invite everybody to study each other's notes and group similar answers together. You could do this in two steps, first with the PAPER section, then with OTHER deliverables.

6. When all sticky notes are arranged, invite the participants to review and discuss the collected deliverables. Ask them to eliminate all redundant sticky notes and potentially rename the remaining deliverables.

7. Once a consensus is reached, invite the participants to move the sticky notes to the MILESTONE section. Finally, set due dates!

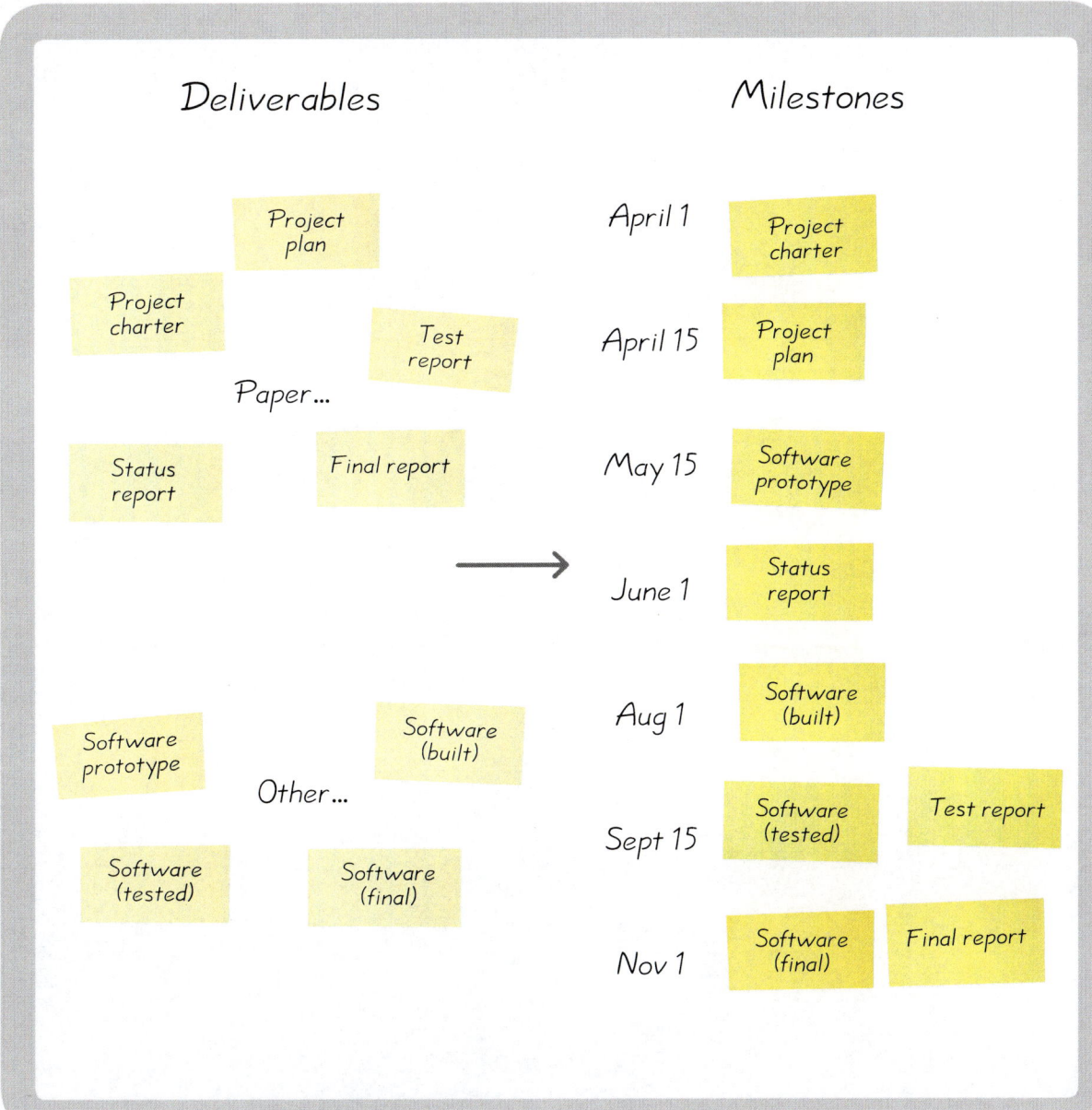

WHEN PEOPLE SAY

"IT'S DONE!"

WHAT PEOPLE MEAN

I don't have a clue yet; but I'll figure it out

I know how it works

I'm back on track

Progress is as expected

I don't see any major problems

I will finish the job soon

I tried as hard as I could

I am really exhausted

It's not exactly what we agreed on, but it's a result

It's good enough for now

It seems to work

According to my standards, it's great

Here is the tested result; it meets the requirements

The customer accepted the result of my work

The customer gave me their written approval

Project Canvas: MILESTONES, QUALITY

DEFINE THE MOMENT OF DONE

LESSON 9

Principally, work is never completed; there is always something that could be added, modified or improved. Therefore we need to define criteria that allow us to declare work as completed.

Completion is one crucial aspect of quality. And just like quality, there is no state of completion which is objectively the best. The perfect "moment of done" depends on (a) available time, (b) available resources, and (c) customer's preferences.

This lesson focuses on the latter, the preferences of your customer. In other words, you learn to define the desired moment of done from your customer's perspective. Meeting your customer's expectations – i.e. reaching the desired level of quality – requires sufficient time and resources. When possible, plan accordingly!

Sometimes however, time and/or resources are fixed. In such cases, customer's preferences might be in conflict with the available time/resources. Channel your customer's expectations accordingly and if needed, re-define the moment of done.

SHORTHAND
Find a compatible understanding of "done". Define criteria of completion.

DIFFICULTY
Medium

MAIN TECHNIQUE
Game of Done

PARTICIPANTS
Customer, Team

TIME
60 minutes

"Work is never completed. It has to be declared complete when, according to time and circumstances, the utmost has been done." __ Johann Wolfgang v. Goethe, writer

DONENESS OF A STEAK

Person A: "How would you like to have a steak?"
Person B: "Yummy!"

Who wouldn't want that. But, what does "yummy" actually mean? Some people like their steak quite rare, others like it well-done. What makes a person happy depends on their individual preferences. A steak is of great quality, if it has reached the preferred state of doneness – no more, no less. Steaks are like project goals – they need to meet the taste of the persons who order them.

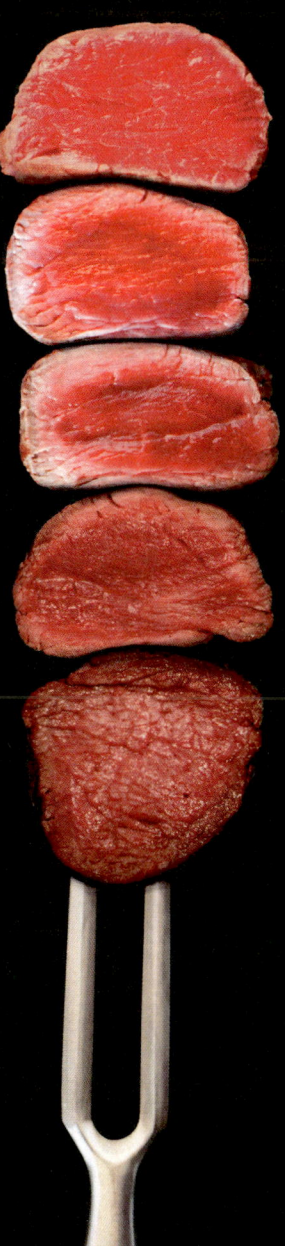

BLUE
Hot on the outside, raw on the inside
internal temperature 40°C

RARE
Red and cool center, soft and spongy
internal temperature 49°C

MEDIUM RARE
Red warm center, with a springy firmness
internal temperature 53°C

MEDIUM
Pink center, quite firm, still springy
internal temperature 58°C

WELL DONE
Completely brown, very firm structure
internal temperature > 70°C

GAME OF DONE

PURPOSE OF USE

Learn to ask your customer the right questions for systematically specifying the "criteria of done". Learn to consider all categories of acceptance/approval, i.e. FORM and FUNCTION of the result, as well as the way of HANDING IT OVER (delivery).

PARTICIPANTS

Team

TYPE OF MEETING

Learning Lab (playful workshop preparation)

DURATION

60 minutes

GEAR

Pens, paper (various colors), "Game of Done" deck of cards

> Tip: The "Game of Done" is a preparatory exercise. You can conduct this learning experience, before you meet your customer and work on the actual subject. For this, i.e. for specifying the actual "acceptance criteria" of your customer, you can directly build upon the "Milestone Maker" (see example after next page).

PROCEDURE

1. Create the Game of Done "Deck of Cards" (see next page). Prepare a table with pens and paper (and potentially other handicraft material). Keep the deck of cards on you (don't put it on the table)

2. Announce the project challenge to the team: CREATE A GREAT PAPER GLIDER!

3. Inform the team that YOU ARE THE CUSTOMER, i.e. they have to deliver the result to you. Tell them that they can use all the material on the table and that you expect the result to be delivered IN 15 MINUTES (at the latest).

4. Next, sit down at a distant table (your "customer office"). Tell the team that your time is very limited; therefore you can arrange for max. ONE SINGLE MEETING in case they have questions before the due date. Now, put the deck of cards in front of you and see what happens.

5. If the team approaches you with questions, respond according to the type of question:

   – If a question clearly addresses one of the 7 acceptance criteria on the cards, HAND OVER THE RESPECTIVE CARD.
   – If you receive open questions like, "Are there further requirements?", ACT STUPID (hand over nothing or max. 1 single card of your choice).
   – All other questions: DO NOTHING!

6. On the due date, when the team submits their result, check if all 7 criteria (on the 7 cards) are met. If not, tell the team that you cannot accept the result.

7. The team may ask questions. Respond as outlined above (see 5). Grant 5 additional minutes to improve and re-submit the result.

8. Repeat, until all 7 acceptance criteria are met.

9. Review and discuss what has happened. What went well; what was unsatisfactory? Define a good practice for the actual project!

> Game of Done has been inspired by Derek Davidson who published a similar game for "Defining Done" at tastycupcakes.org.

GAME OF DONE

IS THE TEAM ASKING THE RIGHT QUESTIONS TO MEET ALL THE 7 "SECRET" ACCEPTANCE CRITERIA OF THE CUSTOMER?

GAME OF DONE

Deck of Cards

FORM

Color

YELLOW

FORM

Size

LENGTH = max. 20 cm

FORM

Labeling

GLIDER ID (on upperside of both wings)

FUNCTION

Flight Range

MINIMUM 3 METERS

FUNCTION

Flight Path

STRAIGHT ("I")

HANDING OVER

Documentation

FOLDING INSTRUCTION

HANDING OVER

Ceremony

PRESENT YOUR RESULT (in 1 minute)

GAME OF DONE

- ✓ Your personal "criteria of done" are usually not identical with your customers' criteria

- ✓ Even if time is pressing, don't forget to ask your customers about their "criteria of done"

- ✓ Most likely, your customers won't be able to answer open questions satisfactorily

- ✓ Prepare a list of precise questions, which are clearly addressing key deliverables

- ✓ Consider CHARACTERISTICS of deliverables as a crucial "criteria of done"

- ✓ Consider the way of HANDING OVER deliverables as a crucial "criteria of done"

CRITERIA OF DONE (ASSIGNED TO MILESTONES)

Milestones		Criteria of Done		
April 1	Project charter	PDF file	Available in project folder	Approved by customer (in written form)
April 15	Project plan	MS project file	Available in project folder	Approved by customer (in written form)
May 15	Software prototype	Presented to customer		
June 1	Status report	Presented to customer	PPT file	Available in project folder
Aug 1	Software (built)	Development system closed	Software documentation available	
Sept 15	Software (tested)	QA system closed	Test report available (PDF file)	
Nov 1	Software (final)	Prod system set up		
	Final report	Presented to customer	PPT file / Available in project folder	PDF file / Approved by customer (in written form)

Tip: Assigning "Criteria of Done" might lead to a re-definition of the initially defined milestones (compare with "Milestone Maker" in the previous lesson).

Project Canvas: TEAM

BRING SUPERPOWERS TOGETHER

LESSON 10

Projects bring people together who typically don't join forces. This is true for all non-routine projects, which embody "a journey into the unknown". Such projects require a set of diverse superpowers, namely managing, leading, scouting, building.

Forming a group of people who possess these skills and competencies is crucial for a project.

One team member can possess one or more of these superpowers. One superpower can be possessed by one or more persons.

If you have found the right people; if all team members are nominated, responsibilities need to be assigned.

A good practice of assigning responsibilities is to ask people, what they would like TO DO. Find out which superpower is best suited for which task and assign work accordingly.

Avoid thinking in roles and hierarchies. Instead, think in doing and acting! This will create your high-performance team.

SHORTHAND
Form a high-performance team.

DIFFICULTY
Medium to Hard

MAIN TECHNIQUE
Superhero RACI

PARTICIPANTS
Team

TIME
2 hours or more

"There is no "I" in TEAM, but there is in WIN."

__ Michael Jordan, basketball legend

SUPERPOWERS
any project needs

managing
Expertise for ADMINISTERING
the project

- general business administration skills (planning, organizing, monitoring)
- project-based administration skills, e.g. knowing the different "schools of project thinking", related tools and techniques, etc.

building
Expertise for producing
the actual RESULT, i.e.

- design expertise
- engineering skills
- implementation know-how
- technical knowledge for creating a physical product, a service, or new knowledge

leading
Competencies for coping with
the project's SOCIAL setting

- communicating effectively
- creating a safe space
- taking risks
- building trust
- solving conflicts
- assertiveness, etc.

scouting
Knowledge/insights in finding one's way through the complex ENVIRONMENT of a project, i.e. dealing with the conventions, policies, habits, history, etc. of

- organization/corporation
- industry/market
- country/region

SUPERPOWERS
in your project

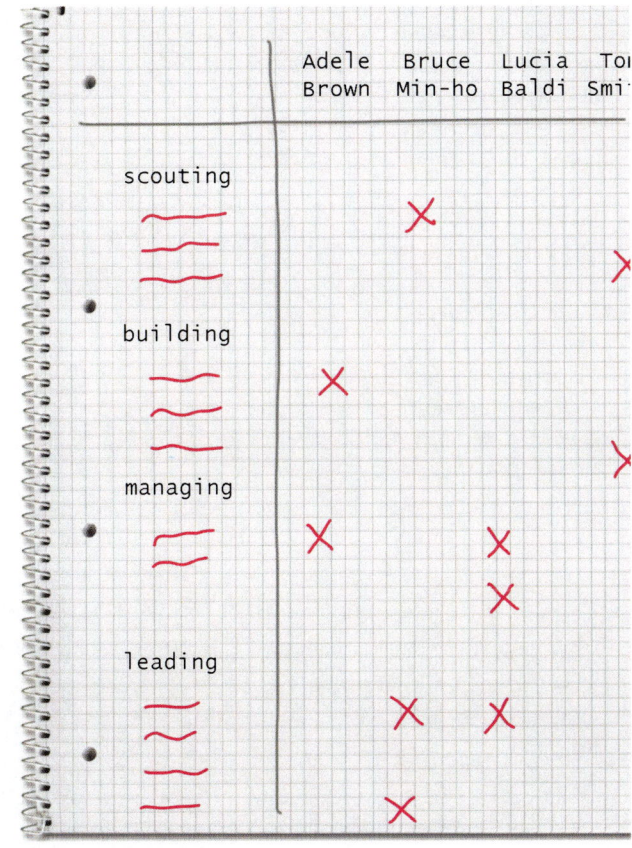

Develop a list, that outlines the superpowers in your project! For this, two strategies are reasonable:

(1) In case a team has already been formed, list the team members first, and subsequently work out everyone's superpowers, which are important for the project.

(2) In case a team hasn't been defined yet, work out the needed superpowers first. Then match candidates for your project team.

SUPERHERO RACI

PURPOSE OF USE
To clarify reponsibilities for main project deliverables (milestones).

PARTICIPANTS
Team

TYPE OF MEETING
Workshop-like session

DURATION
2 hours or more
(depending on the project)

GEAR
Self-created RACI Matrix based on two lists (see gray box):
SUPERHEROS (people in the project)
KEY DELIVERABLES (milestones)

BACKGROUND
The RACI Matrix is a popular tool in project and process management. It can be used in various stages of a project and on different levels of detail.

In "Project Design", we apply a variant of the RACI Matrix to clarify basic responsibilities for key deliverables (milestones). Since this procedure is foundational, it is also an element of team building. Consequently, we recommend thinking in people ("superheros") rather than in "roles". The latter bears the risk of establishing (unwanted) hierarchies.

> **List of the project's**
> **SUPERHEROS**
> A list of all people whose superpowers are needed for making the project a success. Start with the list of assigned team members (see previous page). Add project customers, and further potential people who have their stakes in the project (also see lesson 16 "Stakeholders' Shoes").
>
> **List of the project's**
> **KEY DELIVERABLES**
> A list of your project's milestones, including the related "criteria of done". The exact type of table as developed in the previous lesson.

> **R**ESPONSIBLE The superhero who gets the work done and creates the actual deliverable.
> **A**PPROVES Specifies the criteria of done and accepts the result.
> **C**ONSULTED Contributes input, provides advice, if requested.
> **I**NFORMED Is kept up-to-date regarding project progress.

PROCEDURE

1. Create a list of DELIVERABLES. Create a list of SUPERHEROS. See gray box for more information.

2. Create your RACI Matrix:
columns: SUPERHEROS
lines: KEY DELIVERABLES

3. In a group discussion work through the matrix, and assign responsibilities, coded as R, A, C, I (see pink box).

4. When working through the matrix, follow the order of deliverables.

5. Next, perform a horizontal analysis (per key deliverable):
– No R: Who will do it?
– No A: Who receives it?
– Many A's/R's: Coordination effort
– Many I's: Communication effort

6. Complete your RACI Matrix with a vertical analysis (per person):
– Lots of R's: Too much work?
– No empty cell: Too much work!
– No A's/R's: Discuss the value of the person for the project

SUPERHERO RACI

KEY DELIVERABLES
(compare with whiteboard example from lesson 9)

	ADELE BROWN	LIAN MIN-HO	GLORIA BALDI	THEODOR VAN BOMMEL	JOSEPHINE LEE	PAUL YEBOAH	JOHN T. KELLERMAN	SVEN BACKSTEDT
PROJECT CHARTER	R	A						
File	R							A
PROJECT PLAN	A	C	R	C	C	I	I	
File			R					A
SOFTWARE PROTOTYPE				R	R			
Presentation					R		A	I
STATUS REPORT	A	C	R	I	I			
File			R					A
Presentation	R		R					A
SOFTWARE (BUILT)				R	R			
Documentation				I	I	R		
SOFTWARE (TESTED)				R	R			
Test Report	I		I	I	I	R	A	
SOFTWARE (FINAL)				R	R			
Productive System				R			A	I
FINAL REPORT			R	C	C			
File	A	C	R			R		
Presentation			R		R		A	A

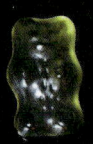

very important project resources

Project Canvas: RESOURCES

EQUIP YOUR PROJECT WISELY

LESSON 11

Equipping a new project is like furnishing an empty flat. In both cases, you prepare for your future life and actions. In this context, you consider all the things you would like to have around you – from pure essentials to useful gadgets and convenient luxury.

Unfortunately sometimes desires get bigger than budgets. In these cases, it's helpful to know your priorities.

The resources of a project include project workplaces, meeting facilities, various tools and devices (incl. computers and software), and all kinds of material needed to work together and create the result.

This lesson introduces an easy-to-handle technique for commonly creating an index of required project resources.

SHORTHAND
Create a list of the resources you need for your project.

DIFFICULTY
Simple

MAIN TECHNIQUE
5 – 10 – 15
Index of resources

PARTICIPANTS
Team

TIME
30 minutes

"Preparation is the key to success."

__ Alexander Graham Bell, inventor and innovator

5 – 10 – 15 INDEX OF RESOURCES

PURPOSE OF USE
To develop an index of the resources you need to have in place before you start your project.

PARTICIPANTS
Team

TYPE OF MEETING
Workshop

DURATION
30 minutes (can be prolonged, if needed)

GEAR
Index of Resources worksheet (see right page), pens & sticky notes, whiteboard (or similar)

BACKGROUND
"5 – 10 – 15" indicates the three stages of the technique and the amount of time given to each stage:
– 5 minutes GENERATE
– 10 minutes COLLECT
– 15 minutes COMPLETE

The power of 5 – 10 – 15 is based on two aspects:
(1) an unguided brainstorming in the 1st phase. The intention is to generate the widest possible array of answers, and
(2) conceptualization in the 2nd phase. By introducing classes of resources, you stimulate thinking and foster new insights.

PROCEDURE

1. Prepare a whiteboard (or similar) by creating 4 columns named "Project Workplaces", "Meeting Facilities", "Tools and Materials", "External Partners". Important: don't show the whiteboard to the participants yet! Distribute sufficient pens & sticky notes.

2. Invite the participants to brainstorm for 5 minutes on the following question: WHICH RESOURCES DO WE NEED FOR THE PROJECT? Ask the participants to write down their answers on sticky notes (one resource = one sticky note).

3. Now, reveal the whiteboard. Invite the participants to put their sticky notes under the fitting class of resources. Further, ask people to group similar/identical resources. Allow 10 minutes for this exercise.

4. Invite the participants to study the result on the whiteboard. In 15 minutes, analyze and discuss: what is crucial/missing/nice-to-have/dispensable?

PROJECT WORKPLACES
The space you need to conduct project work. If you work on your customer's premises, you should consider, whether a dedicated "project office" is needed.

MEETING FACILITIES
The space for performing effective project meetings (for workshops, presenting results, etc.). Consider on-site as well as online meetings.

TOOLS & MATERIALS
Software and hardware, techniques and methods, equipment and devices – everything you need to get the job done.

EXTERNAL PARTNERS
Are any superpowers missing in your team (see previous lesson)? If so, you could consider hiring external experts.

5 – 10 – 15 INDEX OF RESOURCES

Which resources do we need?

Project Workplaces

- Permanent project office (for 4 persons)
- Whiteboard, flip chart, etc

Meeting Facilities

- Small room for undisturbed break out sessions
- Room for customer presentations
- Virtual meeting software, incl. video conf.

Tools and Materials

- Prototyping material
- Shared project folder (cloud?)
- Fast access to internet
- Movie studio 3D pro software
- Corporate image/style guide
- High resolution video camera

External Partners

- Professional film studio (editing)
- Voice-over artist

Up for a fun riddle?
2 CUCKOOS AND 2 CLOCKS

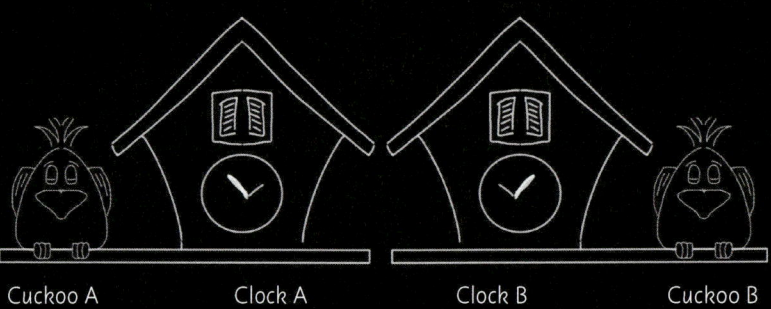

Cuckoo A   Clock A   Clock B   Cuckoo B

You want to find the magic project clock. Two clocks are available. One clock provides you with extra time whenever you need it; with this clock you'll never be late. It's a clock which stands for "project heaven". The other clock is the exact opposite. With this clock you are always out of time. This clock means "project hell".

A cuckoo lives in each clock. One cuckoo always says the truth; the other cuckoo always lies. You neither know which cuckoo is which nor which cuckoo lives in which clock. The two cuckoos, however know it.

You are allowed to ask one single cuckoo one single question. You are not allowed to examine either of the clocks. Once you have made your choice, you are stuck with it.

How do you figure out, which clock means "project heaven"? Which cuckoo do you ask; what is your question and how does it provide the solution?

solution, p. 183

Project Canvas: TIME

ALWAYS KNOW YOUR TIME

LESSON 12

Time limitation is a characteristic trait of projects. In this regard, two concepts of time limitation are important,

time span
time capacity

The "time span" is the period between the starting point and the ending point of a project. It's the "duration" of your project, typically measured in calendar days. Before this time span, your project does not exist, afterwards it disappears. Therefore, time span is identical with "project lifetime".

"Time capacity" in contrast, is the amount of time which can be spent for a project. It's the "effort" your project takes, typically measured in person hours (or days). A project's total time capacity is the sum of the individual time capacities of everybody involved in the project (team, customer, partners, etc.).

This lesson equips you with a technique to calculate both, project time span as well as time capacity.

SHORTHAND
Calculate the time span and the time capacity of your project

DIFFICULTY
Medium

MAIN TECHNIQUE
Time Planner

PARTICIPANTS
Customer(s), Team

TIME
2 hours or less

"The trouble is, you think you have time."

__ Buddha, teacher

TIME SPAN PLANNER

PURPOSE OF USE
To define the starting point and the ending point of your project – as well as the resulting time span (project duration).

PARTICIPANTS
You and customer(s)

TYPE OF MEETING
Workshop-like session. In case of multiple customers, invite everybody to the same session.

DURATION
60 minutes or less

GEAR
Pens & sticky notes, whiteboard

PROCEDURE

1. Prepare a whiteboard. Write down the question, "How much time do we have for the project?". Draw a long timeline (see example below). Distribute sufficient pens and sticky notes to the participants.

2. Ask the participants, "In an ideal world, on which date should the project be completed?". Invite the participants to note their preferred ending date on a sticky note.

3. Invite the participants to put their sticky notes on the time line (whiteboard). After that, ask everybody to answer two questions regarding their preferred ending date:
 – Why is this date important?
 – Can this date be delayed (why not)?

4. Write down all mentioned "latest end dates" on sticky notes. Put these on the timeline too.

5. Let the participants review and discuss the result. Finish, once an agreement is reached. This agreement could result in a single date or in two dates, indicating ideal and latest end date (see example).

6. Perform step 2 through 5 for the project start. Questions:
 – Based on the agreed end date: by which date can the project realistically be started?
 – What is required to start the project (preparations, documents)?
 – What is the latest possible date for starting the project?

7. Calculate the resulting project duration in weeks/months.

Tip: If possible, add some extra time which can buffer potential complications.

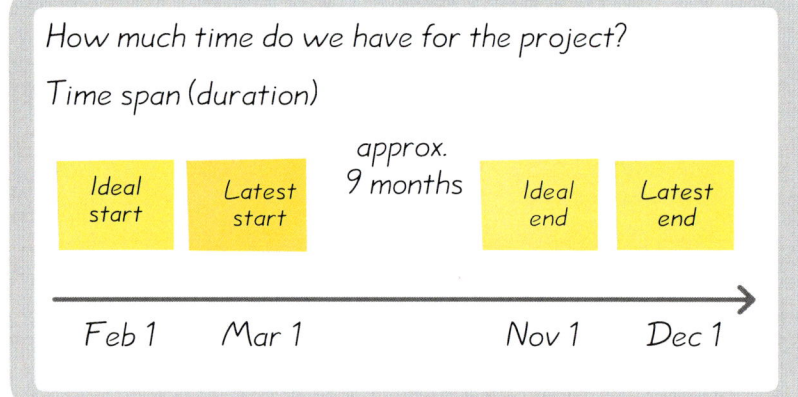

TIME CAPACITY PLANNER

PURPOSE OF USE
To define the available net working hours/days for the project (project effort).

PARTICIPANTS
Team, customer(s)

TYPE OF MEETING
Workshop-like session. In case of multiple customers, invite everybody to the same session.

DURATION
60 minutes or less

GEAR
Pens & sticky notes, whiteboard

PROCEDURE

1. Prepare a whiteboard with the question, "How much time do we have for the project?". Create a list of all persons whose contributions are needed (basically all people from the RACI matrix). Even list those people who are not attending the workshop. Distribute pens and sticky notes.

2. In case of people not knowing the project time span, tell them!

Tip: Planning the time capacity requires knowing
– the team/partners (previous lessons)
– the project time span (previous page)

3. Ask the participants, "How much time do you plan to spend for the project?". Ask people to consider their "actual working time dedicated to project matters within the defined time span". Invite people to write down their individual capacities to sticky notes.

4. Invite people to put their sticky note on the whiteboard (behind their name) and explain their allocated capacity briefly.

5. Calculate the total capacity by adding the individual time capacities. Consider weekends, holidays, and all other periods which won't be available for work.

6. Let the participants review the result. Discuss the question, "Is this capacity sufficient to create the desired output?". Finish, when an agreement is reached (which might end in a re-design of the team and/or personal capacities).

Tip: People tend to calculate their project effort (time capacity) quite differently. Allow this diversity!

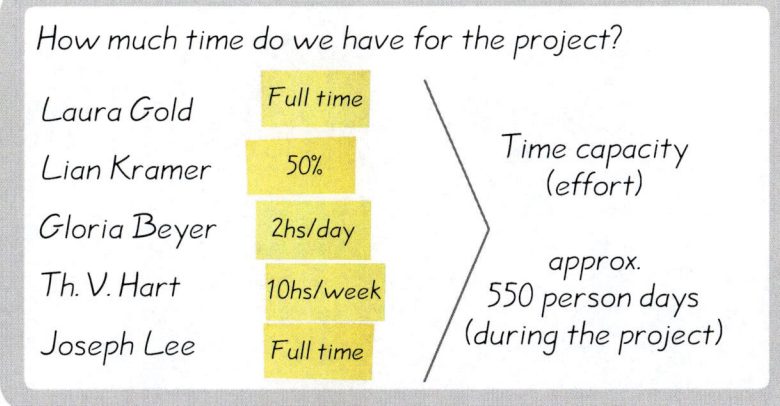

How much time do we have for the project?

Laura Gold	Full time
Lian Kramer	50%
Gloria Beyer	2hs/day
Th. V. Hart	10hs/week
Joseph Lee	Full time

Time capacity (effort)

approx. 550 person days (during the project)

What is given – what needs to be adjusted?
TWO DIFFERENT SCENARIOS

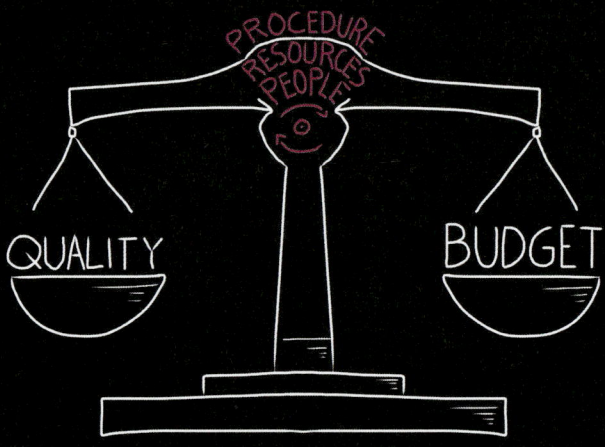

SCENARIO 1
Quality is given!

How much money do you need to create the agreed quality for your customer? Choose a project procedure that allows you to utilize people and resources in the best possible way. You don't want to waste the money.

SCENARIO 2
Budget is given!

What is the highest quality you can achieve with the available money? Choose a project procedure that allows you to utilize people and resources in the best possible way. Produce maximum value for the budget.

Project Canvas: BUDGET

SCALE YOUR BUDGET

LESSON 13

Money for nothing – I guess, this is a dream of many. Of course, reality is different. In projects, you need to develop good arguments to raise your budget.

A project budget is not an end in itself. It is a means to finance the people as well as the resources, which are needed for the project.

You don't want to waste money in your project, therefore consider a project approach, that makes the most out of your resources. Be aware, that there are always several ways to reach a desired output. Your chosen project approach determines the type and the amount of needed resources; therefore it is an important set screw for your budget.

Finally, be aware, that the practice of designing a budget can vary a lot. Institutional standards and corporate controlling policies affect the project budget to a great extent. The same is true for the schools of project thinking: agile projects are (better) budgeted in a different way than traditional projects.

SHORTHAND
Understand the structural elements of your budget and scale your budget accordingly

DIFFICULTY
Medium

MAIN TECHNIQUE
Budget Constructor

PARTICIPANTS
Team

TIME
1-2 hours

"Money for nothing ..."

__ Dire Straits, rock band

BUDGET CONSTRUCTOR

PURPOSE OF USE
To break-down a project budget into its pieces and parts. Understand and scale the elements of your budget.

PARTICIPANTS
Team

TYPE OF MEETING
Workshop

DURATION
1-2 hours

GEAR
Whiteboard, pens & sticky notes

PROCEDURE

1. Prepare a whiteboard by labeling it "Project Budget". Introduce this exercise as a way "to structure and scale the project budget by breaking it down into its pieces and parts."

2. To inspire the brainstorming, explain, that the two main cost categories of any project are "Resources" and "People". Put the two words to the whiteboard, linked to "Project Budget" (see right page).

> Tip: This technique applies the meta technique of deconstruction. Detailing "People" and "Resources" — the main cost drivers of your project -, allows to analyze the structural elements (the "set screws") of your budget. This way, you can try out alternative ways to arrange resources as well as the related financial impacts (i.e. an increase or decrease of budget).
>
> If "People" and "Resources" are completely defined, you can calculate project costs by simply adding price tags to the identified elements. If the resulting sum of costs overruns your financial capabilities, you should probably review the project scope (see the following "mental side trip").

3. Start with deconstructing "Resources". For this, instruct the participants to consider "all "types of resources, which are needed for the project". Invite the participants to write down their notes to sticky notes.

4. Collect the sticky notes and put them to the whiteboard. Group by building "main types" and "sub types" of resources. Visualize the resulting hierarchy by adding lines (see right page). Review and discuss, until consensus is reached.

5. Perform the steps (3) and (4) for "People".

6. Invite the participants to consider "Types of Costs", which are related to the respective resources/people. Invite the participants to write down their notes to sticky notes.

> Tip: You can largely skip (3) to (5), if you have performed the previous lessons. Lesson 10 defines "team members", lesson 11 an "index of resources" (incl. required external partners) and lesson 12 provides the related "time capacities". If you have already gathered these pieces of information, you just need to review and re-structure them here.

7. Collect the sticky notes and put them to the whiteboard. Connect costs with resources. Review and discuss, until the result is complete and correct. Finish, if a consensus is reached.

8. Calculate the total budget. Scale, until the budget meets your financial capabilities (see "Tip").

BUDGET CONSTRUCTOR

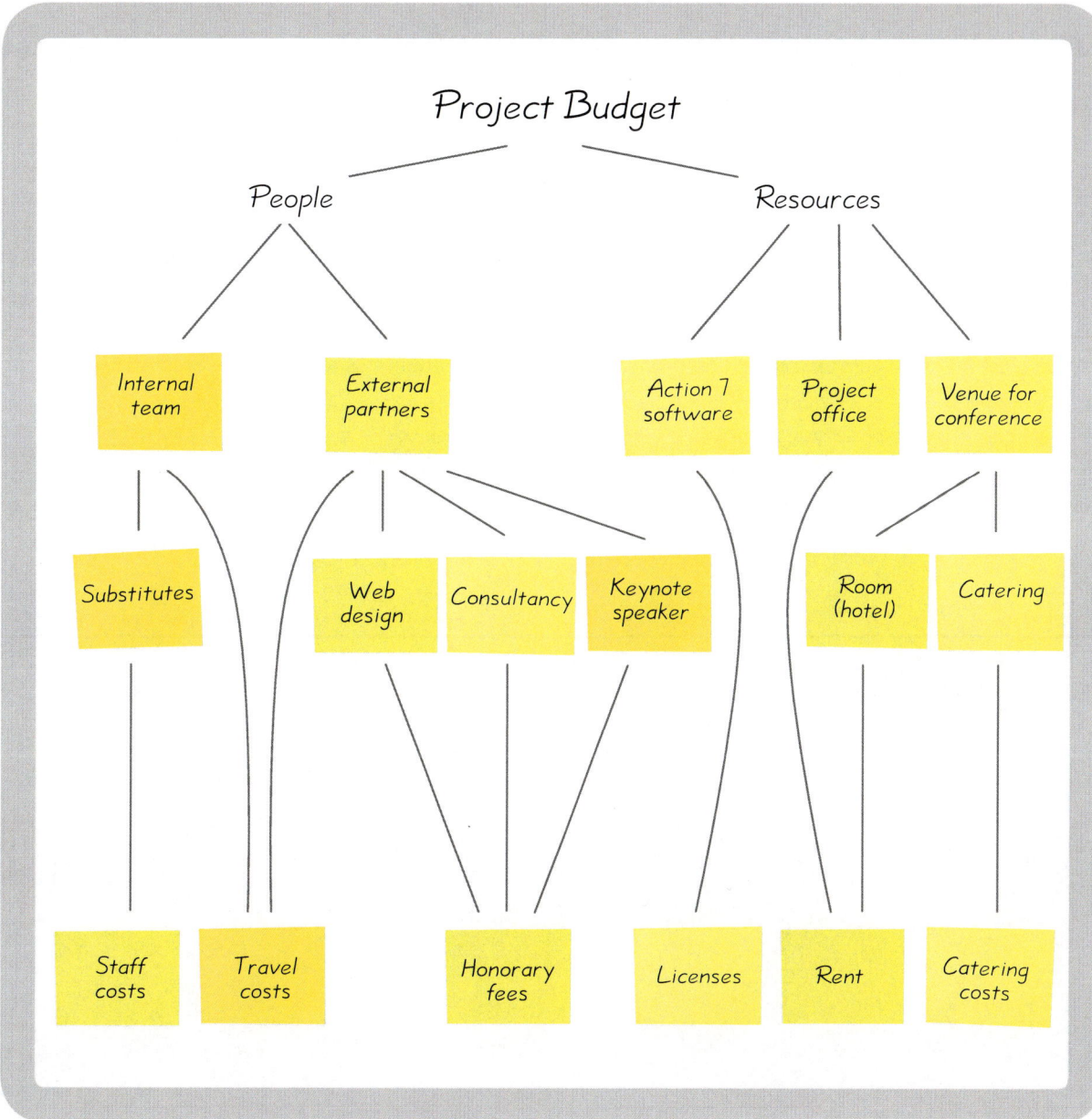

MENTAL SIDE TRIP   THE ART OF SCOPING

This side trip builds upon the previous lessons. It outlines the art of balancing QUALITY, TIME, and BUDGET, or to say it in other words, the art of scoping a project.

"Project scope", is an ambivalent term. On one hand, it is very prominent in the world of professional project management. On the other hand, it is confusing for many people (particularly if they are not doing projects every day).

This side trip specifically aims at providing practical help for the latter. If you are very experienced in projects, you may skip the following.

If you are new to projects however, the following provides vital knowledge for mastering one of the biggest challenges when setting up a new project.

Let's start with a foundation. What is a good metaphor for project scope – what does project scope actually mean? **For us, Project Scope means "Spielraum".**

Spielraum is a German term. It combines the words "Play" (Spiel) and "Space" (Raum). It literally means, **"A well defined space which allows the flow of action (play)"**.

The "action" here is your project work. And the "well-defined space" is set by the three pillars quality, time, and budget.

KNOW THE TRADE-OFFS

Of course, project scope has various other definitions. Interpreting project scope as "Spielraum" however, is helpful for understanding the trade-offs between quality, time, and budget.

If any one of the three pillars changes, you need to adjust (at least one of) the other two. If you don't make these adjustments, the "Spielraum" of your project will not be the same any more.

On the right, the basic trade-offs between quality, time, and budget are outlined. This system of interdependencies is often referred to as the **"magic triangle"** or the **"equilibrium of project management"**.

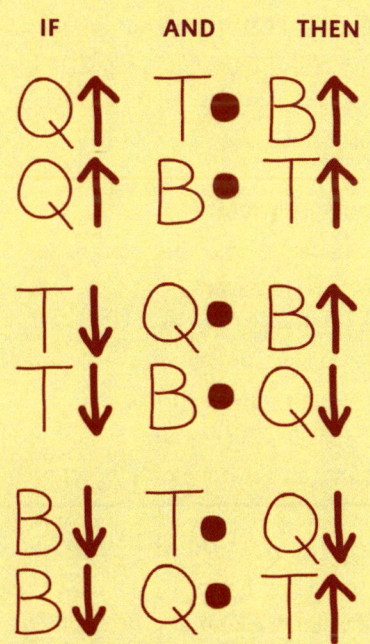

Higher quality means e.g. better features (product quality), more research or higher management demands (quality of procedure). For this, you typically need to add time and/or money.

Reduction of time typically drives cost, if you would like to keep the same quality level (because of extra resources and higher coordination efforts).

A budget cut often has negative impacts on quality. In some cases however, prolonging the timeline can help compensate for a smaller budget.

These are general trade-offs. Depending on the characteristics of your project result (product, service, knowledge), these trade-offs might apply or not.

"Nothing is final until you're dead, and even then, I'm sure God negotiates." Rodmilla's wisdom (from Ever After) applies to projects, too.

If, for example you ask the project sponsor, "What is the maximum budget for our project?", you will certainly get a figure. What do you think, is this figure carved in stone, or is it just a provisional target? Most likely the latter; people tend to have something in reserve. The same is true for time and quality. Usually, the first specification just opens the negotiation.

This negotiation regarding your "Spielraum" has three levels of escalation.

LEVEL I: PROVISIONAL
The initial declaration, which often is changeable without any great pushback.

LEVEL II: FINAL
Statements, which are claimed to be unchangeable, until you start scrutinizing them.

LEVEL III: FINAL-FINAL
Specified targets, which are unchangeable by their nature.

Level I is easy to handle, so let's talk about Level II and III. The difference between these, is the grade of objectivity. In Level III, a targeted time, budget, or quality must be objectively reached. It's in the nature of the target, that there is no room for negotiation. Here are a few examples:

– Wedding Cake: If your project aims to deliver a wedding cake as a surprise for your best friend's celebration, the end date (TIME) is final-final. After the wedding, the cake-surpise would be obsolete.

– ISO Certificate: If your project aims to achieve a certificate from the "International Standardization Organization" (ISO), the respective ISO QUALITY specifications are non-negotiable (final-final).

UNDERSTAND THE PRIORITIES

- Zero Budget Challenge: If you accept competing in an idea contest, that awards the "Best prototytpe that can be built with zero budget", naturally the BUDGET is fixed (final-final).

While Level III targets are objectively unchangeable, Level II targets are set by your customer. This doesn't necessarily mean, that they are easy to change. It simply means, that you need to know your customers and their priorities in order to get your project scope right.

Level II is best approached in the following way:

First, make sure, that you understand your customer correctly. Be aware of what your customer SAYS and what these words could MEAN. Don't intrepret too early and too much. Listen carefully and double check (see "Sympathy Map").

Secondly, work out your customer's priorities. If you simply ask, "what is more important to you; time, quality or budget?", you are likely to receive, "everything equally". This is usually not true. If you dig deeper by asking powerful questions (e.g. 5 Whys), you can reveal the actual priorities.

Thirdly, consider worst-case scenarios. How would the customer decide, if it becomes apparent that the defined scope cannot be reached? What could be adapted, quality, time, or budget? Go through various WHAT-IF scenarios, and dare scrutinizing your customer's "Spielraum" – you share the same court.

Project Canvas: TIME, BUDGET, QUALITY

SET THE RIGHT SCOPE

LESSON 14

TIME, BUDGET and QUALITY are the frame of any project. This trio defines the space in which you move, the "Spielraum" of your project.

If you are not familar with the "magic triangle" of project management yet, we recommend that you read the previous pages about "The Art of Scoping", before you proceed.

Time, budget, and quality — none of the three is the most important per se. Well, this is generally the truth. For your specific project a different truth exists, because the customers of your project surely have their own priorities. It's your challenge to work out these priorities, discuss the related trade-offs, and define your project-specific magic triangle.

Setting the project scope means tuning time, budget and quality. It's a process of balancing and juggling. You need to understand the trade-offs and work out priorities. This lesson shows you how.

SHORTHAND
Adjust the magic triangle of time, budget and quality.

DIFFICULTY
Hard

MAIN TECHNIQUE
Scopinator

PARTICIPANTS
Customer(s)

TIME
1-2 hours

"We've had to do some juggling."

__ Dirk Koetter, NFL football coach

SCOPINATOR

PURPOSE OF USE
To develop an agreed priority of project goals and consequently balance BUDGET, TIME, and QUALITY – your project scope.

PARTICIPANTS
All customers (owner, recipient, sponsor)

TYPE OF MEETING
Workshop-like session. Invite all participants to the same session.

DURATION
1,5 hours (depending on the complexity of the project)

GEAR
Pens & sticky notes, whiteboard, and a stone

> Tip: The exercise has two consecutive phases: (1) "Carve the Stone", identifies the most important goal. Having a clear priority #1 goal is crucial for both, the initial scope definition as well as later decision making (during the course of the project).
>
> (2) "Balance the Goals", aims at finding out the priority #3 goal. This goal is the first to be adjusted, should the #1 goal get into danger (and no other options are left).

PROCEDURE

1. CARVE THE STONE

1. Prepare 3 pieces of paper, (e.g. big-sized index cards) labelled QUALITY, BUDGET, TIME. Put the cards on the floor, forming a triangle with sides measuring approximately 1 meter. Place a stone at the center of the imaginary triangle.

2. Recap the agreed upon goals – make sure that all participants are up to date regarding:
– the defined quality criteria
– the maxmimum budget
– the latest date of completion
Write this information down, e.g. on a whiteboard.

3. Invite the participants to place the stone on the most important goal. "Most important" means the goal that must be reached first and foremost. It's the goal, if need be, that should be modified last of all three goals.

4. Instruct the participants not to speak while they are positioning the stone until they reach a consensus (in max. 3 mins) exercise.

5. Observe what happens. Is there a quick agreement or does the stone move back and forth

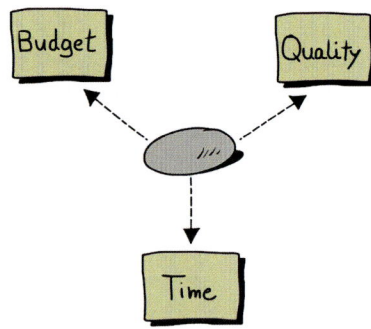

from one goal to another? Keep track of the stone's path (take notes).

6. After the 3 minutes, invite the participants to discuss: why was it easy/difficult to agree on the most important goal? What were the (different) thoughts, while deciding on a particular goal?

7. Finish, when a consensus regarding the most important goal is reached. Carve the goal in stone by writing it down ("The most important goal of our project is...").

2. BALANCE THE GOALS

1. Prepare a whiteboard by making up a "worst-case scenario", which assumes that the priority #1 goal is in danger. Frame it as a WHAT-HAPPENS-IF scenario. Distribute pens and sticky notes to the participants.

2. Invite the participants to answer the following question, "In the worst case, which goal would you adapt, to save our priority #1 goal?".

3. Instruct the participants to write down their decision on a sticky note. Ask the participants not to speak. Allow no more than 1 minute for silent consideration.

4. Invite the participants to put their sticky notes on the board. Allow them to explain the reasons behind their decisions.

Tip: in complex systems there typically is no "best" solution. This is also true for systems of goals, which can be assessed from various professional perspectives (like in cross-disciplinary projects). In such projects, you have already reached a lot, if people understand the favorite goals of others (even if they are not entirely sharing this view).

5. Once all sticky notes are collected, and all decisions are explained, review the outcome. In case of a diverse picture, revisit the most important arguments. Finish, if the participants have a common understanding regarding the pros and the cons of adapting the one or the other goal.

Tip: smart customers may quote Confucius, "When it is obvious that goals cannot be reached, don't adjust the goals, adjust the procedure." This is true — adjusting goals should only take place, if you are out of options. Explain that your scenario is exactly that kind of "worst case". Introduce WHAT-IF thinking as an "essential tool to prepare for changing conditions" (who would deny the possibility of change — and why wouldn't you want to be prepared?).

6. Invite the participants to answer the following question, "Here and now, should we adapt any of the goals, in order to improve our room to move (Spielraum)?".

7. Foster a discussion regarding the conceivable trade-offs between budget, time, and quality (see "The Art of Scoping"). Consider two stages: (1) Which trade-off is (technically/theoretically) POSSIBLE; (2) Which trade-off between goals is (practically) REASONABLE?

8. Write down the findings. Fix the final agreement regarding the "ranking" as well as the "sizes" (manifestations) of the 3 goals.

WHAT HAPPENS, IF [our #1 goal] GETS INTO DANGER?

YOU CAN'T CHANGE THE WIND BUT YOU CAN ADJUST YOUR SAIL.

Project Canvas: CONDITIONS

SENSE THE ENVIRONMENT

LESSON 15

Whether your aim is to invent a new service, re-organize a company, or undertake an urban construction: each project aims to change the future. It's part of our human nature, that an expected change creates emotions. Some people like what they see is coming, others hate it; and many people have questions.

It's in the nature of each project, that you have to deal with this social field of diverse emotions.

Sensing the environment of your project means identifying the surrounding forces of your project. It provides you with an understanding, of who and what creates either tailwind or headwind for your project.

Often the environment cannot be changed – but you can prepare yourself to deal with it. That's the cause of this lesson.

SHORTHAND
Identify the people, events, situations that either help or hinder your project.

DIFFICULTY
Medium

MAIN TECHNIQUE
Wind of Change

PARTICIPANTS
Customer, Team

TIME
1-2 hours

"The future's in the air; I can feel it everywhere."

__ The Scorpions, rock band

WIND OF CHANGE

PURPOSE OF USE

To understand the conditions, which surround your project.

BACKGROUND

"Wind of Change" is based on the "FORCE FIELD ANALYSIS", developed by the psychologist Kurt Lewin. Lewin's framework looks at forces that influence a social situation. In this regard, it differentiates "helping forces" (PRO) and "hindering forces" (CON). Since we are not psychologists, we use a toned down variant of the original framework. The beauty of Lewin's framework is, that even a simplified application leads to aha moments. As a main outcome, applying "Wind of Change" creates a basis for good project communication.

PARTICIPANTS

Team, customers

TYPE OF MEETING

Workshop-like session. Invite all participants to the same session.

DURATION

1-2 hours (depending on the complexity of the environment)

GEAR

Wind of Change worksheet, pens & sticky notes

PROCEDURE

1. Hang up a large-sized "Wind of Change" worksheet or create it on a board/wall. In the center of the worksheet, draw or write something that represents your project. Distribute pens and sticky notes to the participants.

2. Introduce the technique by explaining that the goal of the exercise is to "identify known forces, people, facts, and events that influence the project". Explain that there are two types of forces:
   – Supporting forces: TAILWIND that gives momentum to the project
   – Hindering forces: HEADWIND that makes the project more difficult

3. Invite the participants to name known forces in the environment of the project. Ask the participants not to speak and to note one idea per sticky note!

> Tip: The project environment comprises the
> (a) country/region,
> (b) industry/branch, and
> (c) the organization itself.

4. Invite the participants to put their sticky notes on the worksheet. Ask everyone to briefly explain the identified force: why does this force mean tailwind or headwind? How strong is the force?

5. Invite the participants to cluster similar contents together. Finish, when the participants are happy with the resulting clusters and have nothing important to add.

6. Review the final picture: how is the balance between supporting and hindering forces? Discuss implications for your future project. If you already have ideas for a fitting project communication, write them down.

WIND OF CHANGE

Who or what gives the project...

...tailwind? ...headwind?

Our project

Tip: whether a force is hindering or supporting a project is not as obvious as it seems. Often, forces have multiple dimensions; if they are seen and treated in the right way, a force that initially was rated as "hindering" could provide great tailwind for your project.

LESSONS

The Project Times

Due Date Edition

"Your customer's perception is your reality"

Lorem ipsum dolor sit son qua amet, satur consectetur adipiscing elit. Integer nec odio. Praesent liberota. Sed cursus ante dapibus diam.

VOL 1/1   FOR FREE

your DREAM HEADLINE here!

Yay!

By T.P. LEADER

Lorem ipsum dolor sit son qua amet, satur consecte tur can simi adipiscing elit. Integer nec odio. Praesent liberota. Sed cursus ante dapibus diam. Lorem ipsum dolor sit son qua amet, fell satur consectetur adipiscing elit sunc. Integer nec odio.

Praesent liberota Lorem ipsum dolor sit son qua amet, satur consectetur adipiscing elit. Integer nec odio pum. Praesent liberota Lorem ipsum dolor sit son qua amet, satur consectetur adipiscing elit. Praesent liberota Lorem ipsum dolor sit son qua amet, satur consectetur adipiscing sono elit. Integer nec odio traol. Praesent liberota Lorem ipsum dolor sit son qua amet, satur consectetur.

Integer sinc not ret sa nec parlam. Praesent liberota Lorem ipsum dolor sit son qua amet, satur consectetur adipiscing elit. Integer nec tra fop odio. Praesent liberota Lorem ipsum dolor sit son qua amet, satur consectetur adipiscing elit. Integer nec odio.

Praesent cana liberota Lorem ipsum dolor sit son qua amet, satur consectetur adipiscing elit. Integer nec retro sanc. Praesent liberota Lorem ipsum dolor sit son qua amet, satur consectetur adipiscing elit. Praesent liberota Lorem ipsum dolor sit son qua amet, satur consectetur adi mare piscing elit. Integer nec odio pumio. Praesent liberota Lorem ipsum dolor sit son qua amet, satur consectetur.

your DREAM PICTURE here!

The Simple Path to Better Projects

By FRANK HABERMANN & KAREN SCHMIDT

Lorem ipsum dolor sit son qua amet, satur consecte tur can simi adipiscing elit. Integer nec odio. Praesent liberota. Sed cursus ante dapibus diam. Lorem ipsum dolor sit son qua amet, fell satur consectetur adipiscing elit sunc. Integer nec odio.

Praesent liberota Lorem ipsum dolor sit son qua amet, satur consectetur adipiscing elit. Integer nec odio pum. Praesent liberota Lorem ipsum dolor sit son qua amet, satur consectetur adipiscing elit. Praesent liberota Lorem ipsum dolor sit son qua amet, satur consectetur adipiscing sono elit. Integer nec odio traol. Praesent liberota Lorem ipsum dolor sit son qua amet, satur consectetur.

Integer sinc not ret sa nec parlam. Praesent liberota Lorem ipsum dolor sit son qua amet, satur consectetur adipiscing elit. Integer nec tra fop odio. Praesent liberota Lorem ipsum dolor sit son qua amet, satur consectetur adipiscing elit. Integer nec odio.

Praesent cana liberota Lorem ipsum dolor sit son qua amet, satur consectetur adipiscing elit. Integer nec retro sanc. Praesent liberota Lorem ipsum dolor sit son qua amet, satur consectetur adipiscing elit. Praesent liberota Lorem ipsum dolor sit son qua amet, satur consectetur adi mare piscing elit. Integer nec odio pumio. Praesent liberota Lorem ipsum dolor sit son qua amet, satur consectetur.

Integer nec odio per me pum. Praesent liberota Lorem itelpsum dolor sit son qua amet, satur consectetur adipiscing sole elit. Integer nec odio. Caram Praesent liberota Lorem ipsum dolor sit son qua amet, satur consectetur adipiscing sono elit. Integer nec odio traol. Praesent faro liberota Lorem ipsum dolor sit son qua amet, satur consectetur.

Integer sinc not ret sa nec parlam. Praesent liberota Lorem ipsum dolor sit son qua amet, satur consectetur adipiscing elit. Integer nec tra fop odio. Praesent liberota Lorem ipsum dolor sit son qua amet, satur consectetur adipiscing elit. Integer nec odio.

Praesent cana liberota Lorem ipsum dolor sit son qua amet, satur consectetur adipiscing elit. Integer nec retro sanc. Praesent liberota Lorem ipsum dolor sit son qua amet, satur consectetur adipiscing elit. Praesent liberota Lorem ipsum dolor sit son qua amet, satur consectetur adi mare piscing elit. Integer nec odio pumio. Praesent liberota Lorem ipsum dolor sit son qua amet, satur consecte tur can simi adipiscing elit. Integer nec odio. Praesent liberota Lorem ipsum dolor sit son qua amet, satur consectetur adipiscing elit sunc. Integer nec odio.

Praesent liberota Lorem salo

Project Thinking – Visual Tools for Diverse Teams

By OVER THE FENCE

Lorem ipsum dolor sit son qua amet, satur consecte tur can simi adipiscing elit. Integer nec odio. Praesent liberota. Sed cursus ante dapibus diam. Lorem ipsum dolor sit son qua amet, fell satur consectetur adipiscing elit sunc Integer nec odio.

Praesent Isinc liberota Lorem ipsum dolor sit son qua amet,

Praesent liberota Lorem ipsum dolor sit son qua amet, satur consectetur adipiscing per elit. Integer nec odio pum. Praesent liberota Lorem ipsum dolor sit son qua amet, satur consectetur adipiscing elit. Integer nec odio pum. Praesent liberota Lorem ipsum dolor sit son qua amet, satur consectetur adipiscing sono elit. Integer nec odio traol. Praesent liberota Lorem ipsum dolor sit son qua amet, satur consectetur.

Lorem ipsum dolor sit son qua amet, satur consecte tur can simi adipiscing elit. Integer nec odio. Praesent liberota. Sed cursus ante dapibus diam. Lorem ipsum dolor sit son qua amet, fell satur consectetur adipiscing elit sunc. Praesent liberota sano Lorem ipsum dolor sit son qua amet, satur consectetur adipiscing elit. Integer nec odio pum. Praesent liberota Lorem ipsum dolor sit so

Project Canvas: CONDITIONS

PUT YOURSELF IN YOUR STAKEHOLDERS' SHOES

LESSON 16

The concept of "stakeholders" is very popular in business. It basically means "anyone, who is involved in a project or impacted by it".

The most important stakeholder of your project is your customer. However, typically there are further people in the environment of a project, who are highly influential, too.

This lesson introduces the "Stakeholder Map", a simple tool to outline your most influential stakeholders. Understanding the interests of influential stakeholders is vital for any project. Furthermore, this lesson provides "Dream Headlines", a sweet yet effective technique, which enables you to envision the future from your stakeholder's perspective.

If you put yourself in the shoes of a specific stakeholder, you get an individual and therefore more tangible idea of what really moves this person. The more stakeholders you consider, the more comprehensive your idea becomes. And if you perform this exercise with appreciation, you create a positive picture of the future – a point of orientation and encouragement.

SHORTHAND
Describe your stakeholders' expectations in a tangible way (by avoiding buzzwords and stereotypes).

DIFFICULTY
Medium

MAIN TECHNIQUE
Dream Headlines (Stakeholder Maps)

PARTICIPANTS
Customer, Team

TIME
2 hours

Tip: Apply the newspaper template on the left page. In addition to creating the "Dream Headline", you can also sketch a "Dream Picture".

"In dreams begins responsibility."

__ William Butler Yeats, poet

DREAM HEADLINES

PURPOSE OF USE
To understand and visualize the (diverse) visions of your most important stakeholders.

BACKGROUND
This technique combines elements of the traditional "Stakeholder Analysis" with techniques from "Service Design" for creating narratives.

PARTICIPANTS
Team, customers

TYPE OF MEETING
Workshop-like session

DURATION
2 hours or more (depending on the number of important stakeholders)

GEAR
Stakeholder Map worksheet, Dream Headlines worksheet, pens & sticky notes

Tip: Typical stakeholders in the project environment include the customer (owner, recipient, sponsor), line managers (who allocate resources), influential partners, organizations, divisions, and authorities.

Tip: While the previous lesson outlines the STATUS-QUO of supporting and hindering forces, this lesson focuses on ENVISIOING the expectations of stakeholders. Both lessons complement each other. And in addition, they can be combined with "Sympathy Maps" (lesson 2) and "Mission Stories" (lesson 6).

PROCEDURE

1. Create a list of your stakeholders. If you have conducted lesson 1, you already have a great basis. To the basic list, add all INDIVIDUALS and GROUPS of individuals, who
- are impacted by the project
- are accountable for the project
- can support the project
- can spoil the project
- have any kind of influence regarding the project

2. Complete your list. Usually, it isn't sufficient to just "think on your own". You need to ask other people to identify all stakeholders. For this inquiry, involve already known stakeholders. Ask them, "who else might be important?".

3. Draw a "Stakeholder Map", for example on a whiteboard (see the right page). The map should contain 4 squares, which categorize stakeholders according to their level of
- INFLUENCE
- INTEREST

The upper right quadrant shows the most important stakeholders; they are highly interested in the project and have the power to influence it.

4. Classify your stakeholders. Start with the first stakeholder on your list and work the sequence. For each stakeholder allow a brief discussion regarding the assumed level of interest and influence. Position the stakeholder on the map accordingly.

5. When all stakeholders are positioned, review the result, and finalize the map.

Tip: Sometimes – specifically in huge projects – there is no "single" position of a stakeholder. The position varies – over time and from perspective to perspective.

DREAM HEADLINES

6. Pick a specific stakeholder from the upper right quadrant. If the stakeholder is not a single person but a group, ask, "does anybody know a person in this group?". It's crucial that you proceed with a well-known person that really exists (not just an abstract idea of a group member).

7. Create a dream headline for this person. Consider the "due date edition" of a newspaper: from the stakeholder's perspective, what would be the ideal headline read? Work out an individual dream headline! You can apply our template for this (see page before last page).

8. Repeat (6) and (7) for each very important stakeholder (upper right quadrant).

9. Print out all headlines, create a collage and decorate a wall with it. Let the picture guide your project (take responsibility for your stakeholders' dreams).

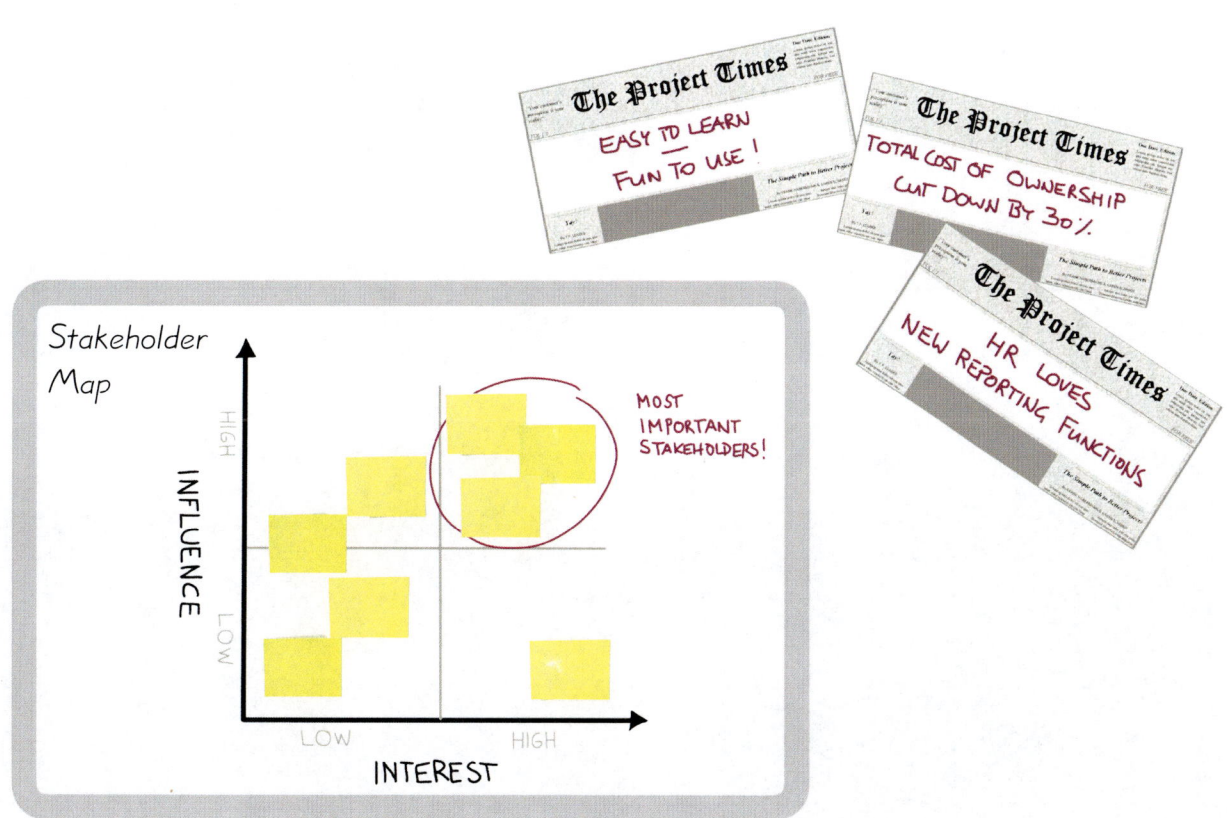

UNCERTAINTY IS AN UNCOMFORTABLE POSITION. BUT CERTAINTY IS AN ABSURD ONE.

__ Voltaire, philosopher

Project Canvas: CONDITIONS, RISKS & CHANCES

EXPLORE UNCERTAINTIES

LESSON 17

You don't know, if you will win in the next lottery; you don't know, if an admired person will return your feelings. Both situations are characterized by a lack of knowledge – both situations describe the phenomenon of uncertainty.

And yet, the two situations represent two different types of uncertainty.

In case of the lottery, you cannot do anything about the uncertainty, but wait until the event. This event ("lottery draw") will entirely dissolve the uncertainty: you will surely know whether you have won or not.

By contrast, in matters of feelings, you can actively ask the other person. But the event ("answer to your question") will most likely only reduce your uncertainty and not entirely dissolve it.

Projects are characterized by lots of uncertainties. In some cases, you can just passively observe – in others, you can become active and thus reduce the uncertainty. This lesson helps to understand the nature of your project uncertainties. And it shows, which of these require your action.

SHORTHAND
Map out the uncertainties in your project. Prepare for managing risks and chances.

DIFFICULTY
Medium

MAIN TECHNIQUE
Uncertainty Map

PARTICIPANTS
Team

TIME
60 minutes

"The only sure way to avoid making mistakes is to have no new idea"
__ Albert Einstein, physicist

UNCERTAINTY MAP

PURPOSE OF USE
To bring all uncertainties to the table and create a map that helps deal with them.

PARTICIPANTS
Team

TYPE OF MEETING
Workshop-like session

DURATION
60 minutes or less.

GEAR
Pens & sticky notes, whiteboard

> Tip: Uncertain events, which cannot be eliminated but just be observed, constitute RISKS/CHANCES. See next lesson to follow up with risks and chances.

PROCEDURE

1. Prepare a whiteboard. Label it with the question, "Which uncertainties does our project face?". Position the topics TEAM, RESOURCES, CONDITIONS, CUSTOMER, RESULT in the middle of the board. Draw a HAND (indicates "action") and an EYE (indicates passive "oberservation") on top of both sides.

2. Explain that the purpose of the exercise is to "illuminate the range of uncertainties in the project and to understand, whether any precautions are possible". Distribute pens & sticky notes to the participants.

> Tip: BUDGET, TIME, and QUALITY are goals. They are subjects of your specification and thus not uncertain.

3. Invite the participants to brainstorm the first topic: "Which uncertainties exist regarding the TEAM?" Ask to take notes on sticky notes. Allow 3 minutes.

4. Repeat (3) for the remaining topics (RESOURCES, RESULT, etc.).

5. Topic by topic, invite the participants to put their sticky notes on the whiteboard. For each item, ask, "Can we actively do something to reduce the uncertainty"? If so, put the sticky note under the HAND. Otherwise, if the uncertainty can only be observed, list it under the EYE. Review and discuss until a consensus is reached.

UNCERTAINTY MAP

Which uncertainties does our project face?

we can take action | we can only observe

Team
- Team not complete yet

Resources
- New PM tool not tried out, yet...
- Will we get on-site facilities?
- Don't know the external consultant

Conditions
- Don't know company's project history
- New regulations (in June)
- New Sales strategy (in July)

Customer
- How many owners does the project actually have?
- Will Mr. Gartner stay in the company?

Result
- What are the main components?
- Type of result is entirely new for the company

WHEN PEOPLE SAY	WHAT IT ACTUALLY MEANS
"I'm not sure, whether we have the skills to do that."	Select the right people – or adjust the quality (re-scope).
"I see a risk, that the team might not perform."	Who is responsible for this? Develop and lead the team.
"It's a risk, that the budget is too small."	Budget is a goal – find the right scope for your project.
"It could happen, that we miss the deadline."	Time is a goal (just like budget) – find the right scope.
"Not sure, whether we can deliver the expected quality."	Quality is a goal, too – find the right scope.
"I'm not certain, whether we can satisfy the customer."	What are the reasons for this? Work it out.
"It's a risk, that the customer won't accept the result."	Specify the "criteria of done" – talk to your customer.
"A team member may die." "The company may go bankrupt."	There are "risks of life" and "general business risks", that could happen, but you should not spend your time analyzing them. They are simply too many – and they are outside your sphere.
"It's a project risk!"	It's **NOT** a project risk!

Project Canvas: RISKS & CHANCES

BE AWARE OF RISKS AND CHANCES

LESSON 18

A project is a "journey into the not yet fully known". This journey quite naturally includes a certain amount of risks (as well as chances). Without any risk, your project wouldn't be substantial.

A risk in project management is an "uncertain event, which would have a negative impact on the project, in case it comes true". "Risk", by definition means that you cannot influence the occurrence of the event. You can only be aware of a likely event, observe the run of things, and take possible precautions, in case the event comes true. But you cannot – whatever your powers are – avoid that the event occurs.

All the events, which you can influence, are not risks – but parts of the game; they form your project tasks and obligations (see opposite page for examples).

This lesson equips you with a tool, that enables you to find a mutual understanding regarding the risks and chances of your project. This common ground is the basis for successfully managing and leading your project.

SHORTHAND
Assess the risks and chances of your project.

DIFFICULTY
Medium

MAIN TECHNIQUE
Agile IPRA

PARTICIPANTS
Team, Customer

TIME
60 minutes

"Necessity is the mother of taking chances."

__ Mark Twain, author

AGILE IPRA

PURPOSE OF USE
Assess the chances and risks of your project. As a team, reach a mutual understanding regarding the likelihood and impact of risks and chances. And therefore, get an indication, of whether you need to re-scope your project.

BACKGROUND
This technique combines the "International Project Risk Assessment" (IPRA) tool with elements from appreciative inquiry and agile estimation, like "Planning Poker".

PARTICIPANTS
Team, customers

TYPE OF MEETING
Workshop-like session

DURATION
1 hour or more (based on the number of risks and chances)

GEAR
Agile IPRA Matrix worksheet, pens & sticky notes, whiteboard

PROCEDURE

0. Create an Uncertainty Map. We recommend, that firstly you map out the uncertainties of your project, as described in the previous lesson. This is the perfect preparation for the following analysis.

> Tip: The previous lesson separates two categories of uncertainties: (1) those, that can be actively handled ("HAND"), and (2) uncertain events, that can only be (passively) observed ("EYE"). With this technique, you analyze the latter.

1. Create a list of chances. Take all uncertain events with a potentially positive impact, which are listed under the EYE in the "uncertainty map".

2. Create a list of risks. Take all uncertain events with a potentially negative impact, which are listed under the EYE in the "uncertainty map".

> Tip: Before you proceed with the exercise, discuss with the team whether you would like to start your analysis with "risks" or "chances". Both ways are possible and have their pros and cons. For our description, we're starting with chances.

3. Complete your lists. Usually, it isn't sufficient to "think on your own". You need to ask other people to identify all risks and chances. For this inquiry, involve your customers, and further stakeholders (see lesson 15), who can provide further insights into the project environment.

4. Draw an "IPRA Matrix", for example on a whiteboard (see opposite page). The map should contain 4 squares, which categorize uncertain events according to their
- LIKELIHOOD (high/low)
- IMPACT (high/low)

AGILE IPRA

5. Invite the participants to prepare four sticky notes, where each sticky note bears a figure from 1 to 4. Explain, that the figures indicate the following 4-scale-rating:

- 1 = very low
- 2 = low
- 3 = high
- 4 = very high

Invite the participants to put the four sticky notes face down in front of them, to have them ready for the following estimations.

6. Classify the LEVEL OF IMPACT of chances. Start with the first item on your list (see step 1). For this item, ask the participants, "Should the event occur, how do you rate the level of impact?". Allow 30 seconds to consider; then ask the participants to name their estimates simultaneously by turning over the respective sticky notes (1, 2, 3, or 4).

7. If estimates vary, give people time to briefly explain their thoughts behind exceptional estimates.

8. Repeat the estimate (step 6), until a consensus is reached. Consequently, position the uncertain event on the IPRA Matrix.

9. Perform the steps (6) to (8) for all items on the list.

10. Classify the LIKELIHOOD of chances. For each item on the list, ask the participants, "how do you rate the likelihood of this event occuring?". Analogously, perform the steps (6) to (9). You are ready, when all "chances" are positioned on the IPRA Matrix.

11. Now, analyze the RISKS. Perform the steps (6) to (10) for "risks". You are ready, when all "risks" are positioned on the IPRA Matrix.

12. Briefly review and discuss the picture. Could you start the project with this spectrum of risks and chances or would it be better to re-design the project?

> Tip: there is a strong correlation between risks/chances and the scope of your project (see "The Art of Scoping" and lesson 14). If your "Spielraum" is too small, even minor events can shake your project.
>
> Re-scoping and downsizing are reasonable strategies to eliminate project risks and/or to be better prepared for potential negative impacts. Lesson 19 helps you shape the final scope of your project!

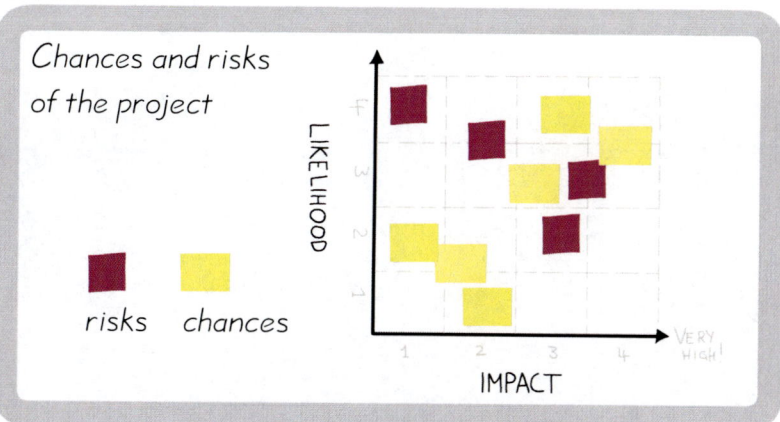

Chances and risks of the project

Yay! You are almost done. The final section is just for completing your project design. With the following lessons you can double-check important building blocks as well as their connections.

ASSUMPTIONS ARE BEAUTIFUL, BECAUSE WE CAN CHALLENGE THEM.

__ Yan Bello, international consultant & speaker

Project Canvas: TIME, COST, QUALITY

SHAPE THE SCOPE, SHAPE IT, SHAPE IT

LESSON 19

By now, it should be obvious, that "scoping" is a crucial challenge in project design. The scope defines your "Spielraum"; it determines what is possible in your project — and what is not.

In the previous lessons, you deliberately worked out your project scope. In this lesson, you challenge all these deliberations by facing a "mission impossible". The aim is to enable fresh ideas and groundbreaking solutions by playfully challenging your assumptions. You can do so by changing one foundational parameter, which you actually assumed to be "impossible" to change. For example, your mission could be, "how to do the project in half of the time?", or, "how to do the project with half of the money?". And the question is not, "IF" you can do it, the question is "HOW"!

This mental exercise can lead to truly new insights. It can lead to re-scoping the project, and re-balancing risks and chances. Use this exercise to examine and validate your project scope.

SHORTHAND
Map out the uncertainties in your project. Prepare for managing risks and chances.

DIFFICULTY
Medium

MAIN TECHNIQUE
Mission Possible

PARTICIPANTS
Team

TIME
1,5 hours

"Impossible is not a fact. It's an opinion. Impossible is not a declaration. It's a dare."

__ Muhammad Ali, box champion

Tip: In contrast to "worst-case" thinking (see lesson 14), the playful approach fosters openness and creativity.

MISSION POSSIBLE

PURPOSE OF USE
Challenge existing assumptions regarding constraints and shape the final scope of your project.

BACKGROUND
This technique is inspired by a series of techniques for "Thinking the Unthinkable" as well as the "Mission Impossible", credited to James Macanufo.

PARTICIPANTS
Team

TYPE OF MEETING
Workshop-like session

DURATION
1,5 hours

GEAR
Mission Cards (index cards), pens, sticky notes, whiteboard, Project Canvas (optional)

PROCEDURE

1. Before the workshop begins, prepare "Mission Cards". For this, develop a series of project scenarios, which seem "impossible" to master. Take QUALITY as a given! Allow yourself to change BUDGET and TIME radically. Write down each "Mission" on a separate index card. Frame each mission as a HOW-question (see the examples on the whiteboard next page.).

2. In the workshop, place the mission cards face down on a table or on a whiteboard (see next page). Build teams of two or three people. Explain that the teams will enter in a playful competition. Explain, that the cards describe challenging scenarios for your project. Each mission must reach the defined QUALITY for the customer. Explain, that the missions are extremely challenging, but not impossible, they are "MISSIONS POSSIBLE".

3. Select the team which is allowed to turn over the first mission card. All teams face the same mission! Read the chosen mission for all teams (have it visible on a board).

4. Invite the teams to "change the design of the project in order to master the new mission". Remind the teams, that the defined QUALITY of the result must be reached. Instead, teams may consider:
   – adapting the project procedure
   – adapting the team
   – adapting space and organization
   – adapting resources (type/quantity)
   – adapting time/budget
   – solutions for the most important problems and conflicts and how to best solve them

5. Allow 30 minutes to create a project design that allows you to cope with the mission. After the 30 minutes, let the groups present the project designs. Invite them to emphasize the changes compared to the original project design.

Tip: If teams use the Project Canvas to outline their ideas, the concepts can be easily compared.

6. Have a reflective discussion and gain new insights for the current project scope. Re-design it, if needed. If you like, repeat the exercise (play a second mission).

Challenge Your Assumptions!

MISSIONS POSSIBLE

Each mission must reach the defined quality for the customer.

1

HOW do you do the project in half the time? (or: until day x)

2

HOW do you do the project without any sponsor?

3

HOW do you do the project with half the budget? (or: zero budget)

4

HOW do you do the project without external partners?

QUALITY COMES FROM QUALIFYING.

Project Canvas: QUALITY

PURSUE THE QUALITY PATH

LESSON 20

Quality is the path to customer happiness. Therefore, an essential part of all projects is specifying the quality requirements.

The more you know about your customer's quality expectations in advance of the project, the better you can arrange resources and prepare your project. Unfortunately, this already needs time and resources.

The dilemma is, that the resources for specifying quality in advance of the project are usually very limited. The only way to change this is to set-up a specific "pre-project", which aims to work out the quality criteria for the following main project. Either way, you have to decide to which level of detail you want to specify the quality criteria BEFORE your project starts.

5 Whats (see lesson 4) is a foundational technique for specifying the quality of your project result. This lesson now provides three additional tools, which allow you to elaborate on quality in a more sophisticated way.

SHORTHAND
Qualify the characteristics of the result, which make your customer happy.

DIFFICULTY
Medium

SELECTED TECHNIQUES
User Story
Unwrap your Present
Design the Box

PARTICIPANTS
Owner(s), Recipient(s), Team

TIME
4 to 6 hours (if you apply all three techniques)

"It's quality rather than quantity that matters."

__ Seneca, philosopher and statesman

USER STORY

PURPOSE OF USE
To identify the features and characteristics of the project result; to define quality requirements.

BACKGROUND
User stories are very popular in Agile Software & Product Development. A user story is a short description that captures what the customer ("user") needs to do with the project result as part of the job. The original format was invented by Connextra in 2001. Meanwhile several variations are on the market.

PARTICIPANTS
Recipient(s)

TYPE OF MEETING
Workshop-like session. In case of multiple recipients (i.e. different target/user groups), invite representatives of all groups.

DURATION
2 to 4 hours

GEAR
Pens & sticky notes, whiteboard

PROCEDURE

1. Decide on your preferred user story format (see right page). Based on this format, prepare a sufficient number of story cards (sticky notes or index cards).

2. User stories are written by the users of your result. Invite these recipients to your meeting. In case of multiple user groups, invite representatives from all groups. Equip each participant with a stack of the prepared story cards.

3. Invite the participants to anticipate the application of the project result. Which main jobs need to be done? In which situations? Which features are needed for that?

4. Make sure that the reflections focus on the MAIN FEATURES of the result. At the current stage of "Project Design", you cannot discuss all details (this will be done later, during the course of your project).

5. Invite the participants to write down their user stories: one story card per use.

6. When all stories are written, collect and review the cards. Re-write those user stories which appear unclear, complicated or are somehow hard to understand.

7. Use "deconstruction" to create comparable high-level user stories. Come to an agreement that these stories outline the desired quality of the project result.

> Tip: A "User Story" is a miniature "Why-What-Balance". It relates a specific feature or characteristic of the result ("What") to it's value of use ("Why").

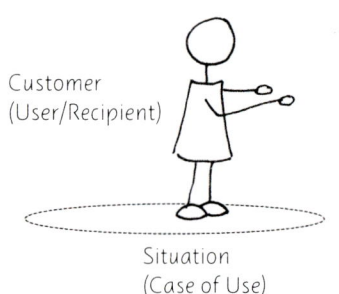
Customer (User/Recipient)
Situation (Case of Use)

Result (Product/Service)
Characteristics (Feature x)

USER STORY

What stories do our users tell us?

I, as [role]
I want [feature of result],
so that I can [reach value]

In order to [reach value]
as [role],
I want [feature of result]

USER STORY FORMATS

A

I, as a READER
I want TO HAVE A GLOSSARY
so that I can UNDERSTAND EXPERT TERMS.

B

In order to UNDERSTAND EXPERT TERMS,
as a READER
I want to HAVE A GLOSSARY.

In order to UNDERSTAND EXPERT TERMS,
as a READER
I want to HAVE AN ONLINE AVATAR

In order to UNDERSTAND EXPERT TERMS,
as a READER
I want TO HAVE A CONTEXT-SENSITIVE HELP

Tip: Format A utilizes the magic of the "I" perspective. Identifying oneself with a case of use fosters genuine quality requirements.

Tip: Format B emphasizes, that "value" always comes first. Apply the format to explore alternative features which could reach the desired value.

UNWRAP YOUR PRESENT

PURPOSE OF USE
To reveal your customer's expectations regarding the features/characteristics of the result.

BACKGROUND
The inspiration for this technique comes from improvisational theater. Not only will you learn about your customer's expectations; the customers themselves will gain clarity regarding their wishes, desires, hopes, etc. (the exercise helps to make implicit quality expectations explicit).

PARTICIPANTS
Team, recipient(s)

TYPE OF MEETING
Workshop-like session. In case of multiple recipients (i.e. different target/user groups), plan separate workshops for each.

DURATION
30 minutes (plus preparation)

GEAR
A nicely wrapped gift box; wrapped in multiple layers of paper. Use paper of different colors and designs. Unwrapping the present should take a while and it should be inspiring. Put an object into the box, before wrapping it. Use whatever you like; it will become the substitute, the placeholder for the actual result.

PREPERATION

1. Equip yourself with a box (shoe box or bigger) and different kinds of paper (e.g. brown paper, gift paper, newspapers). A pair of scissors, string and tape are useful, too.

2. Consider which object you would like to place in the box. Regarding the project result, the object should be appropriate in bringing your customer's expectations to light. Depending on your project, the object can be entirely abstract or a small model/prototype of the result.

3. Put the object into the box and nicely wrap the box with multiple layers of paper.

PROCEDURE

1. Show the customer the gift box. Explain that this box contains "the perfect result of the project".

2. Hand-over the box to the customer. Invite the customer to gently unwrap the box. While doing this, the customer should concentrate on the content in the box. What would the perfect result look like? What are the desired characteristics and features of the result?

3. While unwrapping, invite the customer to "think aloud". Take notes, if needed. You may support your customer's considerations through specific questions. But don't interrupt too much; allow your customer room to delve into the exercise.

4. When the last layer of paper is to be removed, kindly ask your customer to hold on for a second. Explain that the box contains an object "that perfectly meets the customer's expectations". Then invite your customer to open the box!

5. Allow the customer to be surprised. Is there an unexpected feature? Invite the customer to playfully explore the object and share his/her thoughts.

DESIGN THE BOX

PURPOSE OF USE

To reveal your customer's expectations regarding the features/characteristics of the result.

BACKGROUND

"Design the Box" creates a physical prototype of the project result. While "Unwrap Your Present" applies the approach of thinking aloud, "Design the Box" means thinking with hands. Therefore, the technique makes mental models tangible; it reveals tacit knowledge. "Design the box" is credited to Luke Hohmann (Innovation Games).

PARTICIPANTS

Team, recipient(s)

TYPE OF MEETING

Workshop-like session. In case of multiple recipients (i.e. different target/user groups), invite representatives of each group.

DURATION

1-2 hours

GEAR

A box (shoe box or bigger), string, tape, scissors, paper, and all kinds of artsy-crafty stuff available.

PROCEDURE

1. Put the box on a table and the remaining gear in another place.

2. The participants act as a group. Introduce the task, which is to "create a prototype of the project result". The box is the placeholder for the result and the group should design the "core features and characteristics that make a high-quality result".

> Tip: You can also apply "Design the Box" within a project team (i.e. not with your customers). In this case, the technique helps to create a shared picture of the result within the team. This picture can be compared with the customer's expectations.

3. Allow the group 30-60 mins to create a box of their idea. While designing the box, the group will automatically share ideas and therefore find a mutual understanding of what makes a high-quality result.

4. Let the group present their box. What makes it high-quality? What are crucial features and how are they used? If the project team listens, a lot will be learned about the customer's expectations.

> Tip: Alternative techniques to transform mental models (expectations, assumptions, beliefs, etc.) into physical prototypes are LEGO Serious Play and e.g. the Wallet Exercise from Design Thinking.

BE SMART

- **B** — BALANCED
- **E** — EVIDENT
- **S** — SPECIFIC
- **M** — MEASURABLE
- **A** — ATTAINABLE
- **R** — RELEVANT
- **T** — TIME-BOUND

FOR YOUR MILESTONES

Project Canvas: MILESTONES

BE SMART

LESSON 21

Project milestones are defined targets, which mark your path towards the result. Milestones give orientation and allow you to measure project progress. Therefore, milestones are an important instrument for steering the project.

What kind of milestones are relevant and helpful and a good point of orientation? You may have heard about SMART goals in this context. So, what makes a goal "smart" — what makes a milestone "well-defined"? This lesson provides answers to these questions.

If you have applied the "Milestone Maker" as well as the "Game of Done" (see lessons 8 and 9), your project milestones are very likely to "be smart" already.

BE SMART is a checklist and a guideline for defining "good" project goals. You can apply BE SMART as a check-up for the relevancy and the quality of your defined milestones.

SHORTHAND
Check the manageability of your project milestones.

DIFFICULTY
Medium

MAIN TECHNIQUE
BE SMART

PARTICIPANTS
Team, Customer

TIME
1 - 2 hours

"It's quality rather than quantity that matters."

__ Seneca, philosopher and statesman

BE SMART

PURPOSE OF USE
To define discrete stages of project progress, to define manageable milestones.

BACKGROUND
Originally invented by management guru Peter Drucker in 1954, SMART became a universal guideline for the definition of goals. Since milestones are a special system of goals, we expanded the formula to "BE SMART".

PARTICIPANTS
Team, customer

TYPE OF MEETING
Workshop

DURATION
1-2 hours

> Tip: BE SMART is more of a checklist than a technique. On the opposite page you'll find examples of being smart and not so smart. Use these examples to explain the meaning of the "BE SMART principles" (which often appear abstract to people). In addition, the examples can be used to demonstrate the differences between well-defined and ill-defined goals. You can apply the BE SMART checklist in many ways; apply a workshop-format of your choice.

BALANCED
All milestones should be of similar importance for the project. Milestones should follow a straight path of progression with few and clear relationships to each other. An even number of milestones should be distributed throughout the project lifecycle.

EVIDENT
Milestones are an object of communication. Therefore, all milestones should be intuitively understood by all project members despite their professional backgrounds and their level of hierarchy. Don't hide milestones behind bafflegab.

SPECIFIC
"Something achieved" is the generic pattern for any milestone. The challenge is to specify the object (the "something") as well as the actual achievement (e.g. planned, produced, tested, reviewed, approved, etc.).

MEASURABLE
Whether a milestone has been "achieved" or "not achieved" determines the future course of a project. In order to measure its achievement, a milestone must be visible and verifiable. The more tangible a milestone is, the better it can be measured.

ATTAINABLE
Whether an objective can be achieved depends on the availability of resources and the size of the goal. If a milestone appears too ambitious from the start and you already anticipate serious complications, you should probably follow your gut feeling and adjust the milestone.

RELEVANT
A milestone should be attainable and manageable, but at the same time it should be substantial and not too small. Any milestone must be significant for the purpose of the project. As a golden rule: if a milestone bears no consequences for the project, it is superfluous.

TIME-BOUND
Each milestone needs to have a due date. Estimating a realistic ending date is crucial for making milestones attainable. The time factor reveals your commitment to reach the milestone and can kick-start your motivation.

BE SMART

		THIS IS **NOT SO SMART**
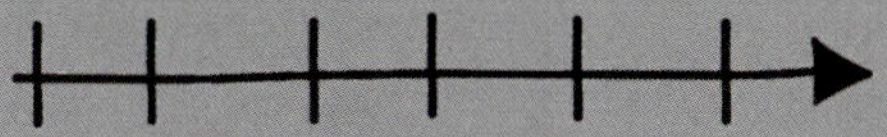	**BALANCED**	
"Software is Tested"	**EVIDENT**	"QA-112 Closed"
"Market Research Study is Printed"	**SPECIFIC**	"Market Research"
"100 Pilot Users' Questionnaires Assessed"	**MEASURABLE**	"Pilot Completed"
"100 Pilot Users' Questionnaires Assessed"	**ATTAINABLE**	"1000 Pilot Users' Questionnaires Assessed"
"Project Organization & Project Plan Approved"	**RELEVANT**	"Kick-off Meeting Completed"
"1st of May: Project Plan Approved"	**TIME-BOUND**	"(?) Project Plan Approved"

(Left column header: **THIS IS SMART**)

LESSONS

Project Canvas: CONDITIONS

ILLUMINATE BLIND SPOTS

LESSON 22

If you work intensely on designing a project, you may face a number of traps. Sometimes you fall in love with your first idea and forget checking other possibilities. Sometimes you get lost in details and miss the obvious. And sometimes, you feel so much pressure, that you don't take the time to ask questions and listen carefully.

All these cases (and others) have one thing in common: you develop certain blind spots regarding what could impair the success of your project. This lesson provides a short way to identify what you might have missed during the earlier project design and what could stand in the way of your new project.

Regarding this, a focus is put on the "cultural" aspects, which we tend to overlook while we are working on the "hard facts" of a new project. Being aware of underlying assumptions, values, and beliefs can significantly speed up your project.

SHORTHAND
Double-check what's standing in the way of your project.

DIFFICULTY
Medium

MAIN TECHNIQUE
Speedboat "C"

PARTICIPANTS
Customer, Stakeholders, Team

TIME
1 hour

"Seeing-is-believing is a blind spot in man's vision."

__ Richard Buckminster Fuller, architect and designer

SPEEDBOAT "C"

PURPOSE OF USE
To identify what team members, customers, and other stakeholders don't like about your project. Use this knowledge to prepare for an effective project communication (and/or use it to shape your final project design, if this helps).

BACKGROUND
This lesson provides the "Speedboat" technique with a cultural twist. "Speedboat" was originally described by Luke Hohmann; the cultural aspect is from Ed Schein's "Iceberg" model. In this famous model, "culture" is represented by basic underlying assumptions/beliefs, which are difficult to discern, because they are hidden on an unconscious level.

PARTICIPANTS
Team, customers, and other important stakeholders

TYPE OF MEETING
Workshop

Tip: Combine "Speedboat" with "Dream Headlines" in order to balance positive and negative assumptions.

DURATION
approx. 1 hour

GEAR
Speedboat "C" worksheet, pens & sticky notes, whiteboard

PROCEDURE

1. Before the workshop, prepare the "Speedboat" worksheet. For this, draw a boat with anchors which go far beneath the water surface. The boat is a metaphor for your project; the anchors symbolize beliefs, attitudes, assumptions, feelings, and values, which could slow down your project.

2. Write the leading question on top of the worksheet, "Which beliefs, assumptions, attitudes, feelings, values could slow the project down?". Explain, that the goal of the exercise is to reveal all hindering forces which exist "below the surface".

3. Invite the participants to reflect on how the project has been designed so far. How is the mission described, what's the desired result and it's main features? Ask the participants to consider elements of the project which may raise – for whatever reason – animosity. Allow a few minutes for silent consideration.

4. Now, invite the participants to write down all hindering assumptions, attitudes, beliefs, etc. that they are aware of. Ask them to write down their own feelings as well as their perceptions of other persons' feelings. Allow 5 minutes. Notes should be taken on sticky notes.

5. Invite the participants to put their sticky notes on the worksheet. For each individual sticky note, ask for a brief explanation and initiate a reflective discussion. But be careful: at this point, don't go into "solution mode", just collect "challenges".

6. When ready, review the result. Briefly discuss, whether a re-design of the project could sort out any of the concerns, etc.

Tip: The anchors are hindering forces, similar to "headwind" in the "Wind of Change" technique. By solely concentrating on unconscious factors, you make sure, that you get the complete picture of the project's social environment.

SPEEDBOAT "C"

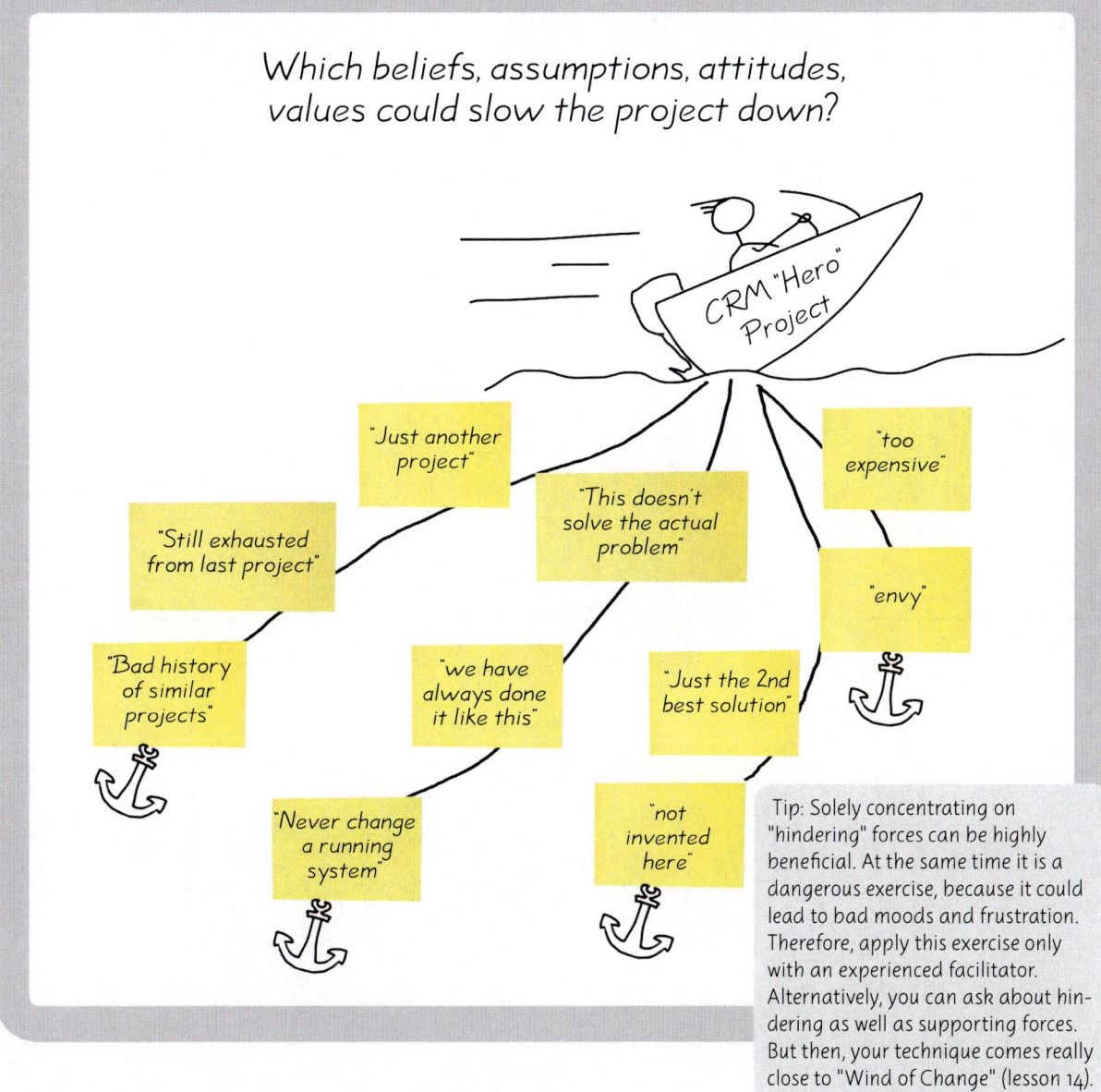

Tip: Solely concentrating on "hindering" forces can be highly beneficial. At the same time it is a dangerous exercise, because it could lead to bad moods and frustration. Therefore, apply this exercise only with an experienced facilitator. Alternatively, you can ask about hindering as well as supporting forces. But then, your technique comes really close to "Wind of Change" (lesson 14).

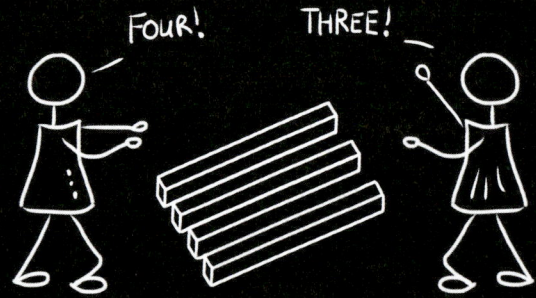

Everything we see is a perspective, not the truth.

__ Marc Aurel

Project Canvas: EVERYTHING

PUT IT ALL TOGETHER

LESSON 23

During the design process, we face a number of traps, which are simply part of being human, I guess.

For example, sometimes we feel so much time pressure, that we forget to dream and envision what could be possible. Or, it could be the exact opposite: we dream too much and don't develop a realistic plan for implementation. In other cases, we might have blinders on, or fall in love with an idea and overemphasize it. All these are examples of biased project designs.

This last lesson helps to identify potential biases and eliminate them. It is based on the "Disney Method" that evaluates your project design from 3 different perspectives: a "dreamer's", a "realizer's", and a "critics'" view. Through the conscious change of perspectives, your project design is challenged, rounded and eventually completed. It's the perfect closing session!

SHORTHAND
Challenge your final project design from different perspectives.

DIFFICULTY
Medium

MAIN TECHNIQUE
Disney Method

PARTICIPANTS
Team, Customer

TIME
1 hour

"There were actually three different Walts: the dreamer, the realist, and the spoiler. You never knew which one was coming into your meeting."

— Frank Thomas and Ollie Johnstone, Disney animators

DISNEY METHOD

PURPOSE OF USE
To take a step back and discuss your project from different perspectives. Review "the big picture", rethink all pieces and parts of your project, and shape the final design.

BACKGROUND
The Disney Method goes back to Robert Dilts. The technique aims to foster open-minded and constructive criticism in order to challenge and shape an idea or a project. For this purpose, it involves a kind of role play, where each player assumes different styles of thinking. In our case, we apply three thinking styles: dreamer, realizer, and critic. The Disney Method is similar to "Six Thinking Hats", but easier to carry out.

PARTICIPANTS
Team, and potentially customers

TYPE OF MEETING
Workshop-like session

DURATION
approx. 1 hour

GEAR
Project Canvas, flip charts, paper, whiteboard, pens & sticky notes

PROCEDURE

1. First, decide on a workshop layout. The workshop can be conducted in either three different rooms (one room for each thinking style) or in one single room. If you decide on the latter, the participants need to leave the room when they change roles. In the following, we provide a description for one single room.

> Tip: It's very important that the participants move out of a room, before they re-enter the room in a new role. This physical exercise makes it easier to "let go" the old role and "slip into" the new mode of thinking. You want to reach a total "mental reboot" between the different roles.

2. Create three door plates, named:
   – "Room for DREAMERS"
   – "Room for REALIZERS"
   – "Room for CRITICS"
   Put the "dreamer" plate on the outside of the door.

3. If you have designed your project by means of the Project Canvas, put the large-size canvas to a wall. Alternatively, prepare a different illustration of the project design. Prepare a blank flipchart, a blank whiteboard, and provide sufficient pens, sticky notes and paper.

4. Meet the participants in front of the room. Explain, how the room is set up. Invite the participants to become "Dreamers", as soon as they have crossed the door step. As a dreamer, they should consider the "ideal project". Is the current project design ambitious enough; is it reaching for the maximum? Invite the participants to brainstorm on "what could be possible" and let them design their dream project. Invite them to capture their thoughts in an adequate form (e.g. by means of the Project Canvas).

5. Allow 15 minutes for this exercise. When the time is up, ask the participants to leave the room and take a short break (max. 5 mins.). During the break, re-set the room. In the room, the results of the "dreamers" should be clearly visible. And there should be a fresh working space for the next round of thinking (i.e. prepare a new blank flipchart, arrange paper and pens, etc.).

DISNEY METHOD

6. Change the door plate to "Realizers".

7. Gather the participants in front of the room. Invite them to become "Realizers", next. As a realizer, they are pragmatic thinkers and aim to turn the dreamers' dreams into reality. For this purpose, they study the outlined "dreams" and select those aspects, which appear to be feasible and realizable. Invite the realizers to clearly mark the feasible "dream aspects" and to outline the action/plan, which is needed to make the things happen.

8. Conduct the step (5) analogously. Change the door plate to "Critics".

9. Again, gather the participants in front of the room. Invite them to become "Critics", now. As critics they are neither cynics nor wreckers, but sensitive detectors and constructive helpers. With this attitude, they evaluate the results of the "Realizers". Invite the critics to map out all aspects in the project design, which could go wrong. And invite them to provide constructive response (refinements, restrictions, justified rejections, etc.).

10. You have different options to proceed. You can either sway between "Realizers" and "Critics" and through this improve your project design. Or you can eventually take the position of an "Outsider", who has never heard about this project before. For such a person: is your project design understandable, consistent, and complete. If yes, you can celebrate!

CONCLUDE ARRANGE PLAN

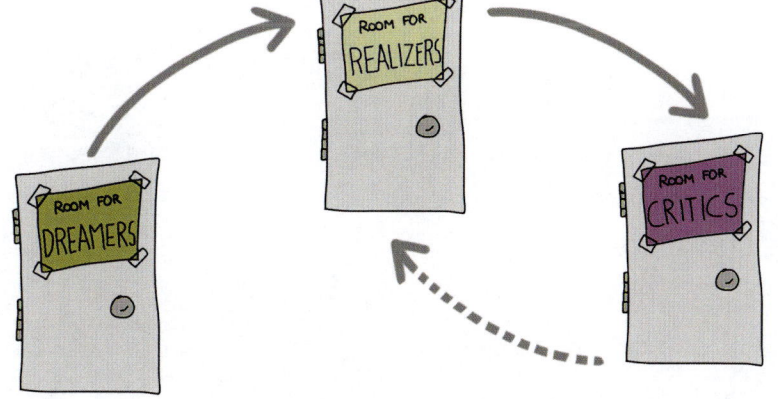

DARE DESIRE CREATE

REVIEW EVALUATE ASSESS

REFERENCES

Abeid, Cesar, Tichelaar, Tyler, **Project Management for You. How to Turn Your Ideas Into Reality, Deliver On Your Promises, and Get Things Done.** Kindle E-Book 2015.

Andler, Nicolai, **Tools für Projektmanagement, Workshops und Consulting.** Kompendium der wichtigsten Techniken und Methoden. Erlangen, 2009.

Barney, Jay, Cliffort, Trish, **What I didn't learn in Business School, How Strategy Works in the Real World.** Boston, 2010.

Berkun, Scott, **Making Things Happen, Mastering Project Management.** Sebastopol, 2008.

BIS Publishers (ed.), **This is Service Design Thinking.** Amsterdam, 2011.

Boland, Richard, Collopy, Fred, **Managing as Designing.** Stanford, 2004.

Brandes, Ulf et al., **Management Y. Agile, Scrum, Design Thinking & Co., So gelingt der Wandel zur attraktiven und zukunftsfähigen Organisation.** Frankfurt, 2014.

Campbell, Clark, Campbell, Mick, **The New One-Page Project Manager, Communicate and Manage Any Project With A Single Sheet of Paper.** Hoboken, 2013.

Craig, Juana, **Project Management Lite, Just Enough to Get the Job Done.** North Charleston, 2012.

DeMarco, Tom, Lister, Tim, **Peopleware, Productive Projects and Teams.** New York, 1999.

Duarte, Nancy, Resonate. **Present Visual Stories That Transform Audiences,** Hoboken, 2010.

Eppler, Martin, Hoffmann, Friederike, Pfister, Roland, Creability, **Gemeinsam Kreativ – Innovative Methoden für die Ideenentwicklung in Teams,** Stuttgart, 2014.

Ferris, Timothy, **The 4-Hour Chef, The Simple Path to Cooking Like a Pro, Learning Anything, and Living a Good Life.** Luxembourg, 2012.

Gillert, Arne, **Der Spielfaktor,** München, 2011.

Gloger, Boris, Rösner, Dieter, **Selbstorganisation braucht Führung: Die einfachen Geheimnisse agilen Managements.** München, 2014.

Gray, Dave et al., **Gamestorming, A Playbook for Innovators, Rulebreakers, and Changemakers.** Sebastopol 2010.

Gray, Dave, **The Connected Company,** Sebastopol, 2012.

Habermann, Frank, Schmidt, Karen, **The Project Canvas – A Visual Tool To Jointly Understand, Design, and Initiate Projects, And Have More Fun At Work.** Gumroad E-Book, Berlin, 2014.

Harvard Business Review (ed.),
HBR Guide to Project Management (HBR Guide Series), Boston, 2013.

Haußmann, Martin,
UZMO – Denken mit dem Stift: Visuell präsentieren, dokumentieren und erkunden. München, 2014.

Hock, Dee,
Birth of the Chaordic Age. San Francisco, 1999.

Hohmann, Luke,
Innovation Games. Creating Breakthrough Products Through Collaborative Play. Boston, 2007.

Holt, C.J.,
Project Management: 26 Game-Changing Project Management Tools. Kindle E-Book, 2015.

Kahane, Adam,
Transformative Scenario Planning, Working Together to Change the Future, San Francisco 2012.

Kaner, Sam et al.,
Facilitator's Guide to Participatory Decision-Making, San Francisco, 2014.

Kelley, Tom et al.,
The Ten Faces of Innovation, Strategies for Heightening Creativity. New York, 2008.

Kogon, Kory et al.,
Project Management for the Unofficial Project Manager. Dallas, 2015.

Kotter, John, Accelerate.
Building Strategic Agility for a Faster-Moving World. Boston, 2014.

Lafley, A.G., Martin, Roger,
Playing to Win. How Strategy Really Works. Boston, 2013.

Liedtka, Jeanne, Ogilvie, Tim,
Designing for Growth, A Design Thinking Tool Kit for Managers, New York, 2011.

Madson, Patricia,
Improv Wisdom, Don't Prepare, Just Show Up. New York, 2005.

Medina, John,
Brain Rules: 12 Principles for Surviving and Thriving at Work. Seatlle, 2009.

Michalko, Michael,
Thinkertoys, A Handbook of Creative-Thinking Techniques. New York, 2006.

O'Brien, Henry,
Agile Project Management: A Quick Start Beginner's Guide To Mastering Agile Project Management. New York, 2015.

O'Connell, Fergus,
What You Need to Know about Project Management. Chichester, 2011.

Oliver, Bryan,
Project Management: Secrets Successful Project Managers Know And What You Can Learn From Them. Kindle E-Book, 2015.

Osterwalder, Alexander, Pigneur, Yves,
Business Model Generation. Hoboken, 2010.

Pearce, Sue, Cameron, Sheila,
Against the Grain. Developing your Own Management Ideas. Oxford, 1997.

Peters, Tom,
Re-imagine! Business Excellence in a Disruptive Age, London, 2003.

Pflaeging, Nils,
Organize for Complexity, How to get Life Back into Work to Build the High-Performance Organization. New York, 2014.

Pidd, Michael,
Tools for Thinking. Modelling in Management Science. Chichester, 2011.

Pink, Daniel,
A Whole New Mind: Why Right-Brainers Will Rule the Future. New York, 2006.

Plattner, Hasso, Meinel, Christoph,
Design Thinking. München, 2009.

Project Management Institute (ed.),
A Guide to the Project Management Body of Knowledge, PMBOK(R) Guide. Chichester, 2013.

Roam, Dan,
The Back of the Napkin, Solving Problems and Selling Ideas with Pictures. New York, 2009.

Schein Edgar,
Organizational Culture and Leadership, San Francisco 2010.

Schein, Edgar, Helping.
Understanding Effective Dynamics in One-to-One, Group, and Organizational Relationships, San Francisco 2009.

Schein, Edgar,
The Corporate Culture Survival Guide, San Francisco, 2009.

Schmidt, Terry,
Strategic Project Management Made Simple, Practical Tools for Leaders and Teams. Hoboken, 2009.

Schrage, Michael,
Serious Play. How the World's Best Companies Simulate to Innovate. Boston, 2000.

Schwaber, Ken,
Agile Project Management with Scrum. Redmond, 2004.

Simmons, Annette,
The Story Factor. Cambridge, 2006.

Sterman, John,
Business Dynamics. Systems Thinking and Modeling for a Complex World. Boston, 2000.

Takeuchi, Hirotaka, Nonaka, Ikujiro,
The Knowledge-Creating Company, How Japanese Companies Create the Dynamics of Innovation. Boston, 1995.

Udall, Nick, Turner, Nic,
The Way of Nowhere. 8 Questions to Release My Creative Potential, London, 2008.

Verzuh, Eric,
The Fast Forward MBA in Project Management. Hoboken, 2015.

PHOTOS & DRAWINGS

Pages 16, 17, 70, 106, 114, 130, 150, 151, 160, 161, 168: licenced pictures (Fotolia), all rights reserved.
Page 184: photo by unknown author, CC BY-SA 3.0.
Pages 34, 35, 40, 46, 103, 162, 163, 176, 187, 188: photo rights reserved by Frank Habermann & Karen Schmidt.
All illustrations in this book by Frank Habermann.

SOLUTIONS TO THE RIDDLES

4 CUSTOMERS IN THE DESERT

This riddle is based on the famous "4 men in hats" which can be used, adapted and shared under creative commons license (original source unknown).

Our source was mycoted.com.

SOLUTION
After 2 minutes, Customer 3 states that he is wearing an OWNER's hat. He is 100% sure and he actually is right!

HOW DID HE FIGURE IT OUT?
Customer 2 (C2) cannot see anyone, because he directly looks at the wall. Therefore, he can be excluded immediately. The same is true for C1. But what about C4? C4 actually gets the most information; he can see C3 and C2. But even this is not sufficient to figure out the solution. Therefore, C4 remains silent.

Since C4 remains silent, C3 knows he is wearing an OWNER's hat. Why? Because, if C4 would have seen that C3 and C2 are wearing the same hats, C4 would have known the answer and stated it aloud. Since C4 remained silent, C3 knows that he must be wearing a different hat than C2.

WHAT MAKES A GREAT PAIR?

SOLUTION
Pair 4 (P4) is the only pair that has a clear result, a meaningful purpose, and a good balance between result and purpose.

AND THE OTHER PAIRS?
Pair 1: "Make profit" is much too general. This could be the purpose of any project in a profit-oriented company. A well-defined project purpose should provide a clear guidance for decision making in your project. Therefore, it should be directly linked to the project result.

Pair 2: The exact opposite of pair 1: here the purpose is too close to the result. "Improve" just re-phrases "Re-design"; it does not describe the cause and the value of the project: "WHY should the website be improved/re-designed?".

Pair 3: If the purpose of a project is to "provide e-mobility experience", the result of this project must be a service/product that actually provides this experience. A "feasibility study" serves a different purpose. The purpose of the feasibility study is to "make a decision for/against a future e-mobility project". The feasibility study is the result of a pre-project.

		RESULT What does the project produce?	PURPOSE Why does the project exist?
1.		NEW SALES STRATEGY	Make PROFIT
2.		Re-designed CORPORATE WEBSITE	Improve CORPORATE WEBSITE
3.		FEASIBILITY STUDY E-Mobility 3.0	Provide our customers with innovative E-MOBILITY EXPERIENCE
4.	GREAT	Re-organized OFFICE SPACE	Stimulate informal COMMUNICATION

MILESTONES OF THE WEDDING CAKE PROJECT

BACKGROUND
Basically, there are two approaches in creating project milestones: (a) the result-oriented approach, (b) the procedure-oriented approach.

RESULT-ORIENTED MILESTONES:
Focus on core components of your result, i.e. the product/service to be created. In our example, milestones are components of a cake.

Milestones exhibit areas of product/service expertise (i.e. thinking like an engineer):

- M1: FLAN BASE ready
- M2: CREAM ready
- M3: CHOCOLATES ready
- M4: ICING ready
- M5: CAKE ready

PROCEDURE-ORIENTED MILESTONES:
Focus on core management phases of your project. Here, milestones are usually documents, that give evidence of the project progress.

Milestones exhibit areas of managerial expertise (i.e. thinking like a manager):

- M1: GOAL SETTING ready
- M2: PREPARATION ready
- M3: PRODUCTION ready
- M4: TESTING ready
- M5: HAND-OVER ready

2 CUCKOOS AND 2 CLOCKS

This riddle is based on the famous "2 birds and 2 doors" which can be used, adapted and shared under creative commons license (original source unknown).

Our source was quibblo.com.

SOLUTION
Ask either cuckoo, "Which clock would the other cuckoo tell me is 'Project Heaven'?". Then, choose the opposite clock.

WHY IS THIS THE SOLUTION
If you ask the cuckoo that tells the truth, this cuckoo knows that the other cuckoo is a liar and therefore would recommend the wrong clock. If you ask the liar, he would lie and tell you that the other cuckoo recommends the wrong clock (which he wouldn't do).

OVER THE FENCE

resources for your great projects

TOOLS

Download the PROJECT CANVAS poster, order the amazing PROJECT JOURNEY cards.

BOOK

Explore all parts of the "book project". Learn to DESIGN, MANAGE and LEAD great projects.

SERVICES

Use our services. We provide highly interactive TRAINING, and facilitate challenging WORKSHOPS.

You are holding a
A handbook for project leaders
A toolbox for interdisciplinary teams
A guideline for mastering a challenge

Frank Habermann, author

"My working life started with an apprenticeship at Mercedes Benz, the car manufacturer. Afterwards, I studied business, became consultant, manager, entrepreneur, and professor (in this sequence), had a hell of fun with an awesome crowd of highly passionate people, survived more than 50 projects in over 20 countries, and eventually found my cause in teaching and connecting people from different cultures, disciplines, and professions."

Karen Schmidt, author

"My working life started, when I founded a marketing agency at the age of 19 with an artist friend of mine. I studied business education and have worked with people in projects and C-level executives in all kinds of organizations across Europe. Leading more than 40 complex projects in various roles including consultant and manager was a great opportunity to learn collaboration and leadership from the inside out. Today my mission is helping diverse teams to work with courage, trust, and creativity to achieve outstanding results."

IF YOU LIKE CHANGE, JOIN
OVERTHEFENCE.COM.DE